THE FOUR CODES OF PREACHING

THE FOUR CODES
OF PREACHING

Rhetorical Strategies

JOHN S. McCLURE

Westminster John Knox Press
LOUISVILLE • LONDON

© 2003 John S. McClure
Published in 1991 by Augsburg Fortress Press.
Published in 2003 by Westminster John Knox Press.

All Scripture quotations are the author's own translation except those noted as RSV, from the Revised Standard Version of the Bible, coyright © 1946, 1952, and 1971 by the Division of Christian Education of the National Council of Churches.

The sermon "Martha Missed Something" is copyright © 1976 Edmund A. Steimle and used by permission.

Excerpts from *The Dark Interval: Towards a Theology of Story* by John Dominic Crossan are copyright © 1998, 1975 Polebridge Press and used by permission.

Interior design: Publishers' WorkGroup
Cover design: Tony Feltner

Published by Westminster John Knox Press
Louisville, Kentucky

This book is printed on acid-free paper that meets the American National Standards Institute Z39.48 standard. ∞

PRINTED IN THE UNITED STATES OF AMERICA

Library of Congress Cataloging-in-Publication Data is on file at the Library of Congress, Washington, D.C.

ISBN 0-664-22806-2

Annie

CONTENTS

ILLUSTRATIONS

PREFACE

This book seeks to break free from constricting homiletical models in order to think strategically about the role of preaching in congregational life. When I was in seminary, students learned to preach in the one-shoe-fits-all school of homiletics. My teachers were, by and large, committed to particular genres of preaching and taught students according to these models. Students who could not fit the shoe were invited (with varying degrees of politeness) to go back to the drawing board or were dismissed as somehow wrong. Like many preachers and homileticians, I grew increasingly dissatisfied with models for sermon design that narrowly conform to master genres of preaching (such as expository, inductive, and narrative), principles of communication theory, the form of the biblical text, or even the more imaginative and ever-elusive form of the gospel.

This book develops a schema for homiletical reflection that attempts to overcome some of the limitations of one-shoe-fits-all homiletics. I have sought to provide a new perspective on preaching derived from the rhetorical study of preaching. I hope that this perspective will help the reader to better understand his or her own homiletical approach and to appreciate the strengths and weaknesses of a wide variety of homiletical strategies.

The problem of subsuming well-known models for preaching within a new schema is that of simply exchanging one kind of shoe for another. I hope that this is not the case. My intention has been to provide a fresh perspective on preaching, not to create a new homiletical master model.

I am also concerned in this book to develop an approach to homiletics that takes seriously the congregational culture in which preaching is situated and the theological role of preaching in that culture. As the reader uses this homiletical schema to discover his or her own homiletical commitments, I suggest a process whereby these commitments can be thought through in relation to the expectations and needs of the preacher's congregation.

This book grows from my conviction that the rhetorical study of preaching can provide some important clues about the role of preaching in congregational life. In order to explore the purposes of preaching in congregations, I have made use of the semiotic theory of Roland Barthes, for whom forms of communication are deeply responsive to and formative of the symbolic life of particular communities of discourse. I realize the limitations of any homiletical approach that purports to be congregation-based but that focuses on the study of congregations indirectly through the analysis of sermon rhetoric. In order to compensate for my sermon-centered approach, I have included, in short form, a congregational analysis component in each chapter; however, the precise nature of congregational analysis for the preacher needs a great deal of further theoretical and practical development.

A further conviction of this book is that the theology of preaching is as much an issue of rhetorical style as it is of rhetorical content. The reader will note that the seeds of a practical theology of preaching are embedded in this book. I did not take the time or space here to flesh out this theology in its fullness.

I have written this book with the working preacher in mind. It is meant to be a tool for the preacher who is in the process of renewing or changing homiletical styles and content. It is also meant to be a tool for the deepening of a preacher's theological leadership in his or her congregation. I use the schema in this book with my basic preaching students, who learn to encode and sequence sermons. They have found that this schema provides a simple way of teasing out their emerging homiletical style and of raising critical questions for their development as preachers. My homiletical supervisors, who lead small preaching groups and do individual sermon reviews, have also found this schema helpful.

Many people have contributed to this book's conception and

development. I owe many thanks to my parents. I learned to appreciate preaching and to hear God's word from the pulpit by listening to my father, M. Scott McClure, preach each Sunday. I learned much about the life of faith from my mother, Margaret McClure; her Sunday lunch discussions of my father's sermons provided the early prototype of my homiletical vocation.

I am grateful to professors at the University of Glasgow, Fuller Theological Seminary, and Princeton Theological Seminary who were patient with me in what must have seemed, at times, my almost cultic interest in structuralism and semiotics. I am especially grateful to Jim Loder at Princeton, who fostered my interest and invited me to explore the potential of semiotics in the study of the epistemological and theological dynamics of worship and preaching.

I am grateful for the patience and support of my good friends at Ensley Highland Presbyterian Church in Birmingham, Alabama, where I was in parish ministry prior to embarking on a career in teaching. More recently I am thankful for the stimulating interaction provided by colleagues and students at Louisville Presbyterian Theological Seminary. The ascent into the real world of ministerial practice and teaching has brought new life and put flesh and bones onto my thoughts.

I am indebted to Louisville Seminary for the sabbatical leave necessary for finishing this project. I am especially grateful for the insights of my friend and colleague Burton Cooper, who gave generously of his lunch and tea times during my sabbatical to help me formulate (in the words of T. S. Eliot) "a hundred visions and revisions, Before the taking of a toast and tea." I am appreciative also of the helpful feedback provided by many others: Steve Hancock, Sally Brown, Jim Hubert, Margaret McClure, Joan Jacobs, David Hester, Marion Soards, and Louis Weeks. In the last months of the project, Melissa Nebelsick's brilliance with computers and word processing brought order and beauty to a disheveled manuscript.

I dedicate this book to my wife, Annie, who has provided support and critical reflection throughout this project and whose love and friendship have made the last thirteen years of my life a profound experience of the grace of God.

RHETORICAL STRATEGIES

She came to me after preaching class with a question: "I have studied the biblical text and I know pretty much what I want to say; now how do I make a sermon out of it?" As she told me what she wanted to say, my mind raced through what I knew about her and the church in which she was to preach, anything that would give me a starting place for an answer to her question. What she was asking me for was a *rhetorical strategy,* a verbal style and approach to her subject matter that would help her communicate with as much intentionality and clarity as possible.

Rhetorical strategies for preaching differ widely and are usually bound to what might be called a preacher's *homiletical profile,* which includes such things as his or her definition of preaching, approach to biblical exegesis and interpretation, facility in language and communication, context of ministry and personal understanding of that context, and any number of other personal interests. Without some knowledge of a preacher's homiletical profile, offering any counsel on how to "make a sermon" is hard. The temptation is to provide a few hard-and-fast rules from general homiletic wisdom within my own ecclesiastical tradition or to offer the preacher a rhetorical strategy that is consistent with my own homiletical profile, but that may be totally unrelated to the homiletical profile of the preacher.

Homileticians usually teach rhetorical approaches that match their own homiletical profiles. If you were to ask me such a question, I might answer you in a variety of ways, depending on my homiletical

1

orientation. For instance, if I am a very rational and didactic person who conceives of the sermon as an exposition of a biblical text, then I may advise you to spend the first half of your sermon teaching the text and in the second half of the sermon apply that idea through examples and analogies. I may tell you to work through the text verse by verse and to teach and apply the scriptural text as you go. I may tell you to derive a theme from the biblical text, divide that theme into parts, show clearly the derivative relationship between each portion of your theme and the biblical text as you move through the sermon, and apply the biblical idea to the life of your congregation as you go.

If, as a homiletician, I am deeply concerned with the relevance of preaching and its interaction with contemporary worldviews, then I may conceive of the sermon broadly as topical. I will invite you to decide upon a provocative topic—usually an existential problem or contemporary issue to which the biblical text relates. I will want you to engage the congregation in an experience of that issue first and then bring theological and scriptural insight to bear on that topic at appropriate points along the way.

If I am fascinated with literary criticism of Scripture, linguistics, or the philosophy of language, then I may see the sermon as the generative center of the world-in-language for the church. I will ask you, first of all, to put aside your sermon idea or theme and ask what the biblical text does rather than what it is about. I may ask you to consider how the genre of biblical literature from which you are preaching functions in human consciousness. I will advise you to frame your sermon in the shape of the biblical text or with a similar performative purpose to that of the biblical text.

If I am interested in the arts and see the sermon as an arbiter between theology and culture, then I may ask you to look for a central image or metaphor within the biblical text. I will ask you to juxtapose that image with images drawn from contemporary literature, drama, film, or your personal experience. I may ask you to string together two or three such images drawn from the Bible, your own experience, and the arts in order to make a sermon.

If I am an avid student of Aristotle's poetics, a disciple of structuralists such as Vladimir Propp and A. J. Gremais, or simply a fan of Alfred Hitchcock, then I will perhaps see the sermon as a creative

plot that enables the congregation to move from the tension of existential irresolution to the insight of theological resolution. I will want
you to plot your sermon first—upsetting equilibrium, creating tension, and then mediating that tension and interpreting the solution in
a theological framework.

An abundance of rhetorical strategies exists for preaching. Indeed,
enough rhetorical approaches are currently on the homiletical market to spark the recent publication of collections of essays by like-
minded authors and at least one book that tries to interpret several
options in homiletical method so that the reader will be able to spot
similarities, differences, and potential pitfalls.[1] These varied conceptions of how to make sermons can be confusing to the preacher. Are
there right ways and wrong ways? Are these approaches mutually
exclusive? Do I have to be a purist or can my own method be a
hybrid? How do I discover which rhetorical approach best fits me
and my situation? How do I fit in, if at all?

THE RHETORICAL SCHEMA

The fundamental purpose of this book is to provide a rhetorical
schema for the preacher or homiletician to use, given a variety of
understandings of what the sermon is and does. A *schema* is a dia-
gram or plan that organizes diverse components in a particular way.
Rhetoric is the purposeful use of verbal language in relation to a
particular audience. A *rhetorical schema* for preaching is meant to
help the preacher organize the diverse verbal components of preaching so that they can be strategically or purposefully effective for a
particular congregation. The rhetorical schema for preaching in this
book is an attempt to organize these components so that they are
useful to preachers who have widely different homiletical profiles. It
is meant to be a schema for developing a sound rhetorical strategy
that is responsive to different conceptions of preaching, various pastoral and social contexts, and a wide range of approaches to the
biblical material.

---

1. Don Wardlaw, ed., *Preaching Biblically: Sermons in the Shape of Scripture* (Philadelphia: Westminster Press, 1983); and Richard Esslinger, *A New Hearing: Living
Options in Homiletical Method* (Nashville: Abingdon Press, 1987).

I am not saying that this rhetorical schema is value-free, ideology-free, or interest-free or that the subject matter of preaching is to be divided into its component parts, like meat and vegetables and spices that are thrown into a large pot without any prescriptive recipe for assembling them to make the best possible stew. In the ensuing chapters, the reader will begin to see clearly how I envision this schema being used and my own basic "recipe" for preaching. However, my main concern is to show how this schema can be used, given any and all approaches or recipes for preaching, to deepen understanding of particular models to which readers may be currently committed or to which they aspire.

This schema can help both homileticians and students of preaching to understand the rhetorical components of preaching in a way that will sensitize them to others who have varying homiletical profiles. The reader can see that one rhetorical strategy may not suit all preachers or contexts for preaching and that hybrid strategies are not only possible but also probable and necessary, given different kinds of preachers and different kinds of preaching contexts. At the same time the reader can see that all rhetorical strategies for preaching gain more depth and breadth when they are implemented self-consciously in relationship to the preacher's homiletical profile and the preaching context.

Using this schema can both promote variety in preaching and deepen the preacher's consciousness of what he or she is doing in sermon preparation. Preachers could conceivably become adept in a variety of rhetorical strategies. I am personally suspicious of any kind of homiletical imperialism that claims to be the only way to preach in the contemporary world or the only biblical method of sermon preparation. Both old and new rhetorical strategies have glaring problems. Homiletics, like theology, art, and science, is always a provisional discipline. It is rooted in a particular epistemological and historical milieu and bears both the good qualities and the limitations of that milieu.

A word here about congregations, traditions, and homiletics is necessary. Congregations cannot be underestimated in their ability to adapt to older, traditional (sometimes even arcane) rhetorical strategies for preaching. Much of public speaking research does not apply to preaching because preaching is done over time, is part of a historically received tradition and ritual, and is only one form of interaction of the several forms of interaction that take place regularly between the speaker and the audience. Preaching is deeply ensconced in particular traditions of communication that congregations recognize and enter into when they walk through sanctuary doors on Sunday mornings. In such circumstances, congregations train themselves to hear in ways that may not meet the newest or most creative rhetorical standards or the criteria of other kinds of communication such as electronic media, drama, or literature. The rhetorical model (however unsophisticated) to which a congregation is accustomed may also ultimately be the one best suited to their theological tradition. Such models can continue to be used with great integrity if they are carefully analyzed from time to time and retooled in relation to biblical hermeneutics, theology, and communication theory.

THE GENRE OF PREACHING

Preaching exists as a unique genre of communication. The word *genre* comes from the field of literature and means simply "a group of texts that bear one or more traits in common with each other."[2] According to the theory of genre, "something that is totally unprecedented is incommunicable."[3] Messages have to be given over to particular genres of communication in order to be communicated. For instance, in order to be sure that my children and I share an understanding of the gravity of a particular misbehavior, we have developed a genre of communication we call a "private talk" in which we both expect, with some brevity (to offset intensity), to be "perfectly clear." When I am watching a basketball game on television, I expect to hear certain things that make up the "announcing" genre of communication, things such as the score, the substitution of various players, and game analysis. Different genres of communication predispose listeners to hear in different ways. In any speech event an implicit communication contract involves the speaker and hearer in a set of basic expec-

---

2. Tremper Longman III, *Literary Approaches to Biblical Interpretation* (Grand Rapids: Zondervan, 1987), 76.
3. Ibid., 77.

tations regarding types and levels of hearing, length, and the kind of participation involved.[4]

To search for these basic communal expectations for the genre of communication that is preaching in the church today, I began the study of sermons, congregational perceptions of preaching, and rhetorical theory that gave birth to this book. Of preachers and sermons I have asked the broad question, What fundamental levels of interaction do most preachers tend to include in their sermons? Of groups of parishioners I have asked the question, What are you listening for when you listen to sermons? More theoretically, I inquired, When preachers begin to speak, how do people decode their speech in order to make sense of it as preaching?

My contention is that the broader Christian community (which includes both parishioners and preachers of most Christian traditions) has a set of minimal expectations, expectations that make a certain kind of speaking event into something that is a sermon, no matter what its rhetorical style or context. Each tradition and congregation accents different expectations and frames those expectations in a particular way, but all of these expectations are present wherever sermons are preached.

To answer students who want to make sermons, I advise them to begin by meeting the minimal public expectations of the preaching genre of communication. At the very least, they have to begin this way if they are to make sense and begin to generate meaning from the pulpit, no matter what their homiletical profile or context of ministry.

Before looking at the basic expectations that constitute the preaching genre of communication, the concept of genre needs some enlarging. It is not a static concept. Genres are not "rigid and pure."[5] Quite often a genre is affected (or infected) by other genres that closely approximate it. Genres have "blurred edges."[6] Therefore, genre studies must always extend the boundaries of the basic expectations that constitute a genre only to the point where those expecta-

---

4. J. Randall Nichols, *Building the Word: The Dynamics of Communication in Preaching* (New York: Harper & Row, 1980), 103–6.

5. Longman, *Literary Approaches,* 78.

6. Ibid., 79, quoted from M. E. Ansler, "Literary Theory and the Genres of Middle English Literature," *Genre* 13 (1980): 389–90.

tions clearly change. At that point the genre of communication itself has changed. For instance, when reporters have just arrived at the scene of an airplane accident, they do not yet have many facts and figures relevant to the accident. What is expected of them is that they report as precisely as possible what has happened and what is happening. When the television anchor begins to ask the reporter for an opinion about the number of casualties or the cause of the accident, however, the basic expectations have clearly changed. We no longer expect facts as we do in the genre of reporting; we expect opinions from the reporter and have shifted to the editorializing genre of communication. Although the edges between reporting and editorializing are sometimes blurred, at a certain point the boundaries of reporting have been pushed to the limit, and we know that what we are hearing is an editorial.

Genres are also historically and contextually conditioned. Although perhaps true at some level of generalization, quite a stretch of categories is required to say that the second-century Greek homily and the twentieth-century televangelist sermon have "one or two" traits in common with each other. When examining a genre, therefore, defining its contextual variations within the margins of a particular time and location is helpful. In our case, the contemporary American sermon principally defines the margins for the genre of preaching under discussion.

Genres also can be perceived at any number of levels of abstraction. Tremper Longman III points out, for instance, how Psalm 98 can be considered generically as "a poem, a cultic hymn, a hymn concerning God's kingship, a divine-warrior victory psalm, and finally as most closely related to Psalm 96."[7] In like fashion, sermons are sometimes classified as expository, topical, pastoral, liturgical, social, and so on. These classifications are really subgenres of the already presumed preaching category of communication. Each subgenre is based on some variable in how sermons are put together: different ways of using Scripture, different ways of using cultural information, different ways of relating preaching to contexts, or different kinds of messages that sermons may have. Because I am interested in explor-

---

7. Longman, *Literary Approaches,* 79–80.

ing what actually makes a communication event into preaching, I will move to a higher level of abstraction in discussing the contemporary American sermon so that I can include these subgenres within a larger framework.

In order to do this, I will introduce two terms, *code* and *intertext,* into the study of preaching. I hope these terms will help to clarify the two principal rhetorical qualities of preaching: (1) that preaching includes several levels of verbal interaction (*codes*) that (2) sponsor several different language-shaped realities (*intertexts*) in congregations.

THE CODES OF PREACHING

A *code* is a system of signs, words, or ciphers that becomes a way of organizing a particular level or aspect of human interaction.[8] All of our interactive experience is coded, that is, shaped or organized in various ways so that we can communicate with more clarity and ease. Codes include verbal (written or spoken) signs as well as nonverbal or kinesic signs. This study will focus on verbal codes from a rhetorical perspective, that is, with a view to their purposeful usage in relation to particular audiences.

Every genre of communication is made up of several different codes. When I approach my good friend in the hallway at the seminary and he has a twinkle in his eye (nonverbal, code of laughter) and pulls me aside (nonverbal, code of camaraderie), saying, "Did you hear the one about . . ." (verbal, code of joke telling), I am already caught up in the various codes that constitute the joking genre of communication. When I go into a restaurant and I am handed a menu, I am aware that my interaction with the kitchen is being organized in a very precise way through the use of clear verbal codes: the code of appetizers, the code of salads, the code of entrees, and the code of desserts.

---

8. Roland Barthes, *Elements of Semiology,* trans. Annette Laver and Colin Smith (New York: Hill & Wang, 1978), 18. See also Roland Barthes, *Mythologies* (Paris: Ed. du Seuil, 1957). The reader should also be aware of the direct influence of Barthes's book *S/Z* (New York: Hill & Wang, 1974) on this entire study. His idea of codes, which he applies to Balzac's short story "Sarassine" in this book, is the model for my study of the codes of preaching.

When people enter sanctuaries and listen to sermons, they participate in the various verbal and nonverbal codes that constitute the
preaching genre of communication. According to my analysis, four
rhetorical codes are fundamental to preaching: the scriptural code,
the semantic code, the theosymbolic code, and the cultural code.

Each chapter of this book explores one of these codes from three
different perspectives: content perspective, intertextual perspective,
and stylistic perspective. A fourth perspective, that of relationship, is
brought to bear on all of the codes at the conclusion of the book,
after the codes have been defined and we can begin to see how they
work together.

Content Perspective

When we look at the codes and intertexts of preaching from the
content perspective, we have to discern what the signs, words, and
ciphers of each code actually are. We ask, What kind of content in a
sermon makes a particular portion or dimension of that sermon scriptural, semantic, theosymbolic, or cultural? As you prepare a sermon
or listen to one, you must be able to recognize each code quickly and
easily.

Sermon *sequences* are defined by the introduction and sustaining
of distinctive, different content in one or more codes. Each sequence
contains shifts among codes. Each sermon sequence may show
flickers of the presence of several codes. When I teach students how
to preach, I request the presence of all four codes in each sequence
when possible (Table 1, p. 10).

Intertextual Perspective

An *intertext* is "a text lurking inside another, shaping meanings,
whether the author is conscious of this or not."[9] According to Robert
Scholes, "Texts refer to other texts. The artist writes and paints, not

9. Robert Scholes, *Structuralism in Literature: An Introduction* (New Haven: Yale
University Press, 1978), 150. Scholes notes: "For Barthes, there is no such thing as a
pure context. All contexts come to man already coded. . . . The great error is to
assume that he is in touch with some ultimate context, while in reality he is simply
transcribing a code."

TABLE 1
Four Codes in Each Sequence

Sequence 1	*Sequence 2*
Theosymbolic code	Theosymbolic code
Semantic code	Semantic code
Cultural code	Cultural code
Scriptural code	Scriptural code

from nature but from his or her predecessors' ways of textualizing nature."[10] To *textualize* means simply to shape in language. Intertexts are "communicative realities" or realities as they exist "in language."[11] When nature is textualized, it is shaped in language in a particular way; it is no longer nature, but nature-in-language. In other words, when Flannery O'Connor encodes the sky as "cloudless" in the final despairing moments of her short story "A Good Man Is Hard to Find," she is textualizing nature. The text of her short story refers to a particular intertext of nature or a style of textualizing nature in fiction. (It might be argued, for instance, that this is an *allusory* style of textualizing nature, or an allusory intertext of nature, since "cloudless" could be taken as an allusion to the second coming, when Christ is supposed to come "on the clouds.") When this happens, the short story sponsors this particular intertext or style of textualizing nature in fiction. By *sponsoring* we mean that the short story (1) vouches for, (2) promotes, and (3) responds to that particular intertext or style of textualizing nature.

Because this book is about the codes of preaching, I will treat each code as a subtext with its own intertext. I will say, for instance, that the semantic code is a subtext in preaching that sponsors an intertext of truth, a way of textualizing truth in the Christian church. Like the artist who writes, not from nature but from "ways of textualizing nature," the preacher preaches not from truth but from ways

---

10. Robert Scholes, *Semiotics and Interpretation* (New Haven: Yale University Press, 1982), 145.

11. See John Dominic Crossan, *The Dark Interval: Towards a Theology of Story* (Niles, Ill.: Argus Communications, 1975), 37. According to Crossan, "Reality is neither *in here* in the mind nor *out there* in the world; it is the interplay of both mind and world in language. Reality is relational and relationship. Even more simply, reality is language."

TABLE 2
Codes and Intertexts

Code	*Sponsors*	*Intertext*
Scriptural		Anamnesis
Semantic		Truth
Theosymbolic		Theological worldview
Cultural		Experience

of textualizing the truth within the Christian church. In other words, an established form of Christian truth becomes an intertext for the semantic code in a preacher's sermons. The semantic code refers to this established intertext for support and legitimation at the same time that the semantic code supports and legitimates the existence of this intertext in the church.

Sermon codes, therefore, do not simply exist in, of, and for themselves. They exist as rhetorical sponsors of particular intertexts. From the intertextual perspective, we will ask of each sermon code, What intertext is this code sponsoring (vouching for, promoting, responding to)? We will define each intertext and suggest what its fundamental characteristics are. Four intertexts parallel the four codes of preaching. The scriptural code sponsors an "intertext of anamnesis," the semantic code an "intertext of truth," the theosymbolic code an "intertext of theological worldview," and the cultural code an "intertext of experience" (Table 2).

The scope of this book does not include investigating at great depth the content and history of the various intertexts of preaching. In this book we will simply identify what these intertexts are, observe their uniqueness in their relationship to preaching, and note the assumptions about those intertexts that show up in the codes of preaching and the kinds of rhetorical impact that preaching has on them.

Style Perspective

As we have suggested, each code exists in a relationship to an intertext. Each code sponsors an intertext in certain ways. The way a code sponsors an intertext is its style of encoding or the style of that code in preaching.

Keeping in mind the three aspects of sponsorship, we will note first of all how each code vouches for its intertext in a certain way. Vouching is a function of the rhetorical space and intensity of the code relative to the whole sermon. A large, conscious, intentional code vouches most strongly for its intertext. For instance, a large, conscious, intentional theosymbolic code vouches strongly for a theological worldview in a particular congregation. It says (1) we have a theological worldview here, (2) it is important, and (3) we are addressing it. When we look at the vouching style, we will look at ways in which the strength or weakness of a code is manifested and what this level of intensity says about the intertext it sponsors.

Second, we will note how each code promotes an intertext in a certain way. A code has a way of saying what kind of intertext it supports. Code style promotes intertext style. A particular style of encoding Scripture promotes a particular kind of anamnesis. A particular style of encoding meaning promotes a particular kind of truth. A particular style of encoding theological symbols promotes a particular kind of theological worldview. A particular style of encoding culture in sermons promotes a particular kind of experience. In each case we will examine code style with an eye to the kind of intertext each code is promoting in the communicational life of a congregation. Preachers are encouraged to make intentional choices of code style based upon theological and pastoral reflection on the intertextual expectations and needs of their congregations.

Third, each code has a way of being responsive to its intertext—of processing residual intertextual expectations, handling plurality, and "negotiating a hearing." The word *negotiation* is very important in considering how communication events are encoded because how sermons are encoded does not depend solely on the preacher. It also depends in large part upon the expectations of the particular congregation within a particular tradition. Expectations have already been shaped in various ways in each congregation. In the best cases, the stylistic contours of the various codes in preaching are not strictly dependent upon the preacher's personal interests. Each code constitutes a rhetorical negotiation between the preacher and those who hear the preacher each week. When this is the case, sermons actually give voice to the compatibilities between the preacher and the congregation while promoting particular kinds of intertexts that meet the theological and pastoral needs of the church.

From the perspective of style, then, we will need to ask first how each code vouches for its intertext. Then we will need to ask what fundamental rhetorical styles each code has in order to suggest what kind of intertext each style seeks to define and promote. Finally, we will want to suggest certain problems in negotiating a hearing, given different intertextual expectations, and how some of these problems can be managed.

Stylistically, I will argue in favor of sermons with strong and strategic styles. I will favor sermons that are encoded strongly and regularly at all four levels (sermons that vouch), sermons that consciously promote intertexts in particular ways for particular theological and pastoral reasons (sermons that promote), and sermons that negotiate each code consciously in relation to other possibilities and expectations (sermons that respond). I expect that such sermons are not only heard most profoundly but also have the ability to lead congregations into relationships with new forms of anamnesis, truth, theological worldview, and experience.

Relationship Perspective

The fourth perspective on the codes of preaching involves us in looking at the relationships that exist between the codes. This topic is saved for the concluding chapter because an analysis of relationships between codes must await further definition of the codes themselves.

From this perspective we will look first of all at how code styles influence the relationships that exist between the codes. Then we will look at the ways that understanding the relationships between codes helps us better understand popular subgenres of preaching such as expository, topical, life-situation, inductive, and narrative preaching. We will see that certain styles of encoding and certain relationships between codes are critical in the definitions of these subgenres of preaching.

We will also begin to see that these subgenres are open to reinterpretation and to expansion. We will see ways that our discussions of content, style, and relationships between codes reveal new insights about emerging subgenres; we may also see the possibility of hybrid approaches to preaching that may be developed to meet the need for new homiletical strategies in an increasingly pluralistic church where congregational expectations are varied and complex.

At the level of the homiletical craft itself, the relationship perspective suggests that preachers can and should consciously order the appearance of each code in the sermonic process, based on theological and communicational decisions. At the very least, conscious and strategic shifts in the relationships between the codes of preaching would enable our congregations to hear the gospel in new, more dynamic ways and provide preachers with a way to craft sermons in a variety of forms.

BEGINNING WITH RHETORIC

To begin my writing in the field of homiletics with a book that starts with preaching at the level of rhetoric perhaps seems to be a backward approach to the subject. Most homiletical texts end with sections on rhetoric after having first dealt with the important issues of the authority and nature of preaching, biblical interpretation, and preaching context. The reason for beginning with rhetoric is, in part, my conviction that these other aspects of homiletics are implicit (if not explicit) in the final rhetorical product of the sermon-in-context and can therefore be examined and explored adequately from the perspective of that end product.

Homiletical education today is sometimes narrowly focused on teaching singular methods (of biblical interpretation and homiletical procedure). My conviction is that preachers need to become practical theologians who can piece together their own homiletical method based upon (1) an understanding of what constitutes the preaching genre of communication, (2) an understanding of their own working style within that genre and what that working style sponsors in congregational life, (3) an understanding of their own congregations' expectations and needs, (4) theological and pastoral reflection on their styles in relation to the expectations and needs of the congregations they serve, and (5) strategic decisions and commitments rooted in that reflection. In its boldest relief, this book provides a schema that may be used as the core of such a process.

More modestly, this schema can be used to develop or better understand a preacher's own working style, or to try my "recipe" to see if it makes sense and is helpful. I hope, at the very least, that this schema will provide the reader a window through which to reflect more deeply on the rhetorical aspects of the preaching ministry.

1

THE SCRIPTURAL CODE

The scriptural code has its historical roots for Christian preaching in the first-century Jewish synagogue. In the synagogue, preaching was bound closely to Scripture and could become little more than a very brief exposition of a biblical text. According to Isaac Levy, "only single verses from the Torah and a maximum of three verses from the prophets could be read before the *Meturgeman* [translator] rendered his paraphrase, lest he become confused and deliver an erroneous interpretation."[1] At the same time, he was "not permitted to speak louder than the reader of the scrolls, thereby displaying deference to the original text, nor was he permitted to prepare a manuscript of his rendering and read it from a written scroll, lest members of the congregation confuse the scriptural text with that used by him."[2] The early roots of Christian preaching show the need to *encode* (put in code) in the sermon as well as in the liturgy a close interpretive and, in some sense, derivative relationship to the sacred Scriptures for preaching.

CONTENT

The content of the scriptural code is any direct or indirect verbal allusion to the words of the biblical text or to the events to which the

1. Isaac Levy, *The Synagogue: Its History and Function* (London: Vallentine Press, 1963), 102.
2. Ibid.

15

biblical text testifies. These allusions can be wide-ranging enough to encompass large portions of Scripture or even the entire gospel story; as such, the scriptural code is virtually unrelated to a specific biblical text. A student of mine who had recently completed a study of fundamentalist preaching remarked, "There doesn't seem to be a specific biblical text for the sermons I studied, really, unless it is John 3:16 or some other encyclopedic text that captures the preacher's fundamental gospel." The sermons were encoded with many scriptural allusions, most of them supporting the evangelist's point, that Christ died for our sins and rose from the dead; therefore, we need to repent, ask forgiveness, and be saved.

By contrast, a particular biblical text may be encoded in such a way that it stands in a precise interpretive relationship with a larger idea or several ideas within the sermon. In such preaching, several details and dimensions of a particular scriptural text are usually engaged rhetorically in the sermon. For instance, at each transition of thought in the sermon, the hearer may be treated to a brief flicker of the scriptural code, indicating some relationship between that new block of thought and the biblical text for the day. In a sermon on Luke 10:38-42, the story of Mary and Martha, the preacher may be focusing on Martha's distraction. We may hear the actual words of the text itself alluded to briefly and abruptly, "But Martha was distracted with much serving," or we may hear these words attributed to Luke, "According to Luke, 'Martha was distracted with much serving.'" There may be further embellishment: "According to Luke, while Mary was sitting at Jesus' feet, Martha was busy serving dinner all by herself. She was distracted by the difficulty and isolation of her task. How can she ever get things ready without some help?"

When we listen for the content of the scriptural code, we are listening quite simply for references of all types to Scripture and to the events to which Scripture bears witness. Any portion of a sermon that has either the scriptural text or biblical events as its fundamental point of reference is part of the sermon's scriptural code.

INTERTEXT OF ANAMNESIS

Liturgists often use the word *anamnesis* to describe a special kind of remembering that is intended to move a sacred person or event from the past into the present, into the here and now. The formal Anamnesis during the Eucharistic Prayer in many Christian traditions always includes some reference to the passion, resurrection, and ascension of Jesus Christ. The recalling of these events during the prayer is meant to make them present and operative in the Lord's Supper.

Like the Eucharistic Prayer and Lord's Supper, preaching is anamnetic.[3] Within every sermon lurks an intertext of anamnesis, a way of recalling the foundational events of the Christian faith. This intertext takes various forms and is found in other aspects of church life as well, including Bible studies, foot washings, Passion plays, prayers of thanksgiving, and devotional prayer groups. Like these events, the sermon invites the congregation into a particular kind of recalling that seeks to make past sacred occurrences, ideas, and stories present in the community of faith.

The sermon sponsors this intertext of anamnesis principally by encoding some kind of interpretive relationship to the stories, life world, language, and events expressed in Holy Scripture. This encoded biblical hermeneutic constitutes the scriptural code in preaching. Preaching contributes this biblical-interpretive quality of anamnesis in preaching to the broader anamnesis of the church. Preaching challenges the church to consider new and changing dimensions of its anamnesis, to grow and change in the ways the church recalls the foundational events of the faith and in the ways the church relates those events to people's lives today. It keeps anamnesis responsive to changing worldviews and historical situations. At the same time, preaching keeps the church's anamnesis rooted in the wider canon of the biblical witness. It is a remembering that will not let us forget the breadth and depth of God's interaction with the people of Israel and the early church.

STYLES

As we noted in the introduction, style has to do with the way each code sponsors its respective intertext. Sponsorship has three compo-

---

3. Geoffrey Wainwright, "Preaching as Worship," *The Greek Orthodox Review* 28 (1983): 325. Wainwright observes that preaching's anamnetic character is caught up in its concern with the historical sense of the biblical text and its ability to ensure a more complete remembering of the history of redemption.

nents: (1) vouching for the intertext, (2) promoting the intertext, and (3) responding to the intertext (negotiating a hearing). With respect to the scriptural code, style has to do with the way the scriptural code vouches for, promotes, and responds to the intertext of anamnesis in the local church.

Vouching for the Intertext

In most preaching today, especially since the revival of biblical preaching and the increased use of preaching lectionaries in mainstream Protestant denominations and in the Roman Catholic Church, the scriptural code is consciously attended to in preaching and strongly vouches for the intertext of sacred remembering or anamnesis in the church. More and more today, preachers are starting with biblical texts in the preparation of sermons rather than with topics, issues, or apologetic concerns. In most cases, biblical texts are read aloud, sometimes at great length, before preaching occurs in worship, and sermons are patently based on portions of what has been read. Most of these sermons refer to Scripture regularly, either through the use of the actual words of the text or through the fleshing out of the text's original or underlying meaning or impact.

Of course, a sermon may have a very indirect style of encoding Scripture. Preachers sometimes say to me, "I got my idea from Scripture and then I left Scripture behind." I recently heard a sermon on the uniqueness of Jesus Christ that used the text "I am the way, the truth, and the life, no one comes to the Father, but by me." During the sermon, the congregation never heard a single direct allusion to the biblical material. The preacher simply read the text and then started preaching about the uniqueness of Jesus Christ by using insights she had gleaned from her exegesis and without referring them to the Bible or to its life world at all.

Even more radically, a preacher may preach a sermon with no biblical text as part of the sermon preparation process, liturgy, or preaching itself. If such preaching is done only occasionally, the congregation, in response to expectations that come with the genre of preaching, will continue to listen for the connections between the sermon and the foundational events of the Christian faith. If it is done week to week, those who expect a recognizable encoding of

Scripture or some reference to the foundational events of the faith will grow frustrated. Others will adjust their idea of what preaching will be from their preacher. Although the scriptural code and the intertext of anamnesis have been distanced in their relationship to the sermon, some hearers will remain convinced that the Bible is still there behind the scenes. Parishioners in such circumstances comment, "I'm sure the Reverend Jones would never say anything contradictory to the Bible," "Many times I have thought about what our preacher said in a sermon while I was reading my Bible on my own," or "Our preacher knows the Bible but just doesn't push it all over us on Sunday mornings."

This last model begins to put preaching into a situation of generic "infection," where it is perilously close to becoming another genre of communication altogether and establishing a different communication contract with the congregation than does preaching. When the intertext of anamnesis is no longer sponsored at all in preaching, the sermon genre has been left behind entirely. Another form of communication has begun.

Promoting the Intertext

Biblical interpretation for preaching has more variety today than ever before. Each way of interpreting Scripture in preaching directly or indirectly promotes a corresponding form of anamnesis in congregational life.

In *The Christian Story: A Pastoral Systematics,* vol. 2, Gabriel Fackre presents a useful set of hermeneutical categories with which we can organize the ways Scripture is alluded to in preaching. Fackre creates four categories to sort out "various ways to bring the [biblical] text into relationship with the context."[4] I will appropriate his categories rather loosely and in some cases very differently. These modes of contextualization—with some simplification and redefinition and with the addition of a fifth category—match the variety of ways in which Scripture is encoded in sermons today. These categories form the five *T*s of scriptural encoding in preaching.

---

4. Gabriel Fackre, *The Christian Story: A Pastoral Systematics,* vol. 2 (Grand Rapids: Wm. B. Eerdmans, 1987), 243.

Translation

Translation means, literally, to "bring over." The first style of encoding Scripture in sermons is translational in nature. Scripture is encoded as original facts, which the sermon is involved in translating (bringing over) into the present. The time that has elapsed between the original and the sermon at hand is unimportant. The translator is more synchronic than diachronic in attitude, seeking out substitutions or equivalencies for words, characters, and ideas that might translate them from the biblical text into the sermonic text.

The translator translates in an almost commonsense fashion primarily what happens in the text or what the text is about rather than what is "behind the text" (its historical, communal, or authorial background) or what is "in front of the text" (its formal, linguistic, or literary qualities). The actual dynamics of that particular scriptural event or discourse are translated into the language of the sermon.

There are three rhetorical substyles of translation. The first is *literal* translation. Here the rhetoric of the sermon wants us to act or think in precisely the same terms that the biblical text wants us to think or act. If the Bible says that the early church "spoke in tongues," the sermon reasserts this as a proposition to be literally translated into the thought and action of the twentieth-century church.

This kind of literal translation, however, is not always possible. For instance, if the preacher is preaching the story of Mary and Martha and the text says that Mary was "seated at his [Jesus'] feet," then the preacher is hard-pressed to get us to replicate this precisely in our thought and action, because, of course, Jesus is not literally present. A literalist would note that *women* in the biblical text should sit at Jesus' feet, because, after all, Mary was a woman. When these literalist impulses begin to distort and limit the meaning of the text, a second kind of translation, called *dynamic equivalence,* takes over. In the dynamic equivalence style of scriptural encoding, the sermon translation is permitted some freedom from the scriptural original in order that it may make better sense. With regard to "sitting at the feet of Jesus," the preacher makes much of the actual practice of having daily quiet moments of sitting (now metaphorically) "at Jesus' feet"—perhaps beneath a portrait of Jesus or a cross, in a sanctuary, or with Scripture in hand—in order to be taught as Mary was being taught by Jesus (the Word). A dynamic equivalentist might equate Mary with all ardent followers of Jesus Christ, both men and women alike, and place the entire Christian community in her shoes.

Those who use dynamic equivalence must permit translation to be ruled as much as possible by the specifics of the actual language of the biblical text itself. The key to dynamic equivalence is that it "retains a determined faithfulness to the intention and structure of the original but at the same time . . . [clarifies] . . . the intention of the text by finding equivalences in the new context."[5]

The freer the translation, the more paraphrastic the equivalencies. Fackre allows for a third model of translation, which he calls *paraphrase*. Here, the translator becomes "more aggressive."[6] In some cases, the sky is the limit. The specifics of the text no longer rule the interpretation. Depending on the translator and his or her community, for instance, Mary and Jesus and Martha might represent any number of things: Mary may stand for all oppressed and marginalized women who typically are forced to sit at the feet of male masters; Mary might become a cipher for "true believers" who spend their time studying the Word and receiving teaching at the feet of Jesus, as opposed to Martha, who, like all social activists, is too busy to hear and respond to the Word.

CONSIDERATIONS

From a hermeneutical perspective the problems that become obvious with a paraphrastic encoding of Scripture are actually problems endemic at every level of this translational encoding of Scripture in preaching. The contemporary hermeneuticist will remind us that we can in no way, given the intervening two thousand years, simply translate ideas from a first-century context into the present day. If you do so, you are paraphrasing from the very start. You cannot help importing into your interpretation your own context-dependent baggage—stereotypes, ideology, theology. We know, by looking at the history of biblical interpretation, about the dangers of allegorization, spiritualization, psychologization, and ideologization

---

5. Ibid., 244–45.
6. Ibid., 244.

that accompany simple translationist interpretations of Scripture.[7] We also know, however, that we have no way to avoid this kind of paraphrastic influence, only ways to subject this influence to critical reevaluations in light of the ongoing analysis of the biblical text in its own historical context and an ongoing analysis of the worldview, life situation, and historical context in the church and world today.

From an exegetical perspective we know also that it is naive to presume that we are always working with a set of historical facts when we are interpreting biblical narratives. A whole set of transmissive, cultural, authorial, and communal factors influence the biblical text in front of us. Getting at "what actually happened" or "what the text is about" is, in many cases, not possible.

We know also the great danger in translating culture-specific and context-specific dictums like rules regarding men's hair length, the wearing of veils, or commands that women should be silent in church into our own culture. In other words, to preach "what happened in the text" or "what the text is about" is not sound exegesis when what is "behind the text" and "in front of the text" is not considered also.

In spite of these and other dangers, most preachers encode Scripture in this translational way to some extent in their sermons, although this may not be the dominant guise for Scripture in their sermons. Whenever obvious comparisons are drawn between the concepts, characters, or actions in the Bible and contemporary experience, the translational scriptural code is voiced in preaching.

One of the strengths of this kind of scriptural encoding of sermons is that it is a very overt, obvious, and derivative usage of Scripture in which congregations actually hear the words of the biblical text itself in the sermon and are invited to reflect on the text's foundational relationship to contemporary life in the Christian community. When Scripture is encoded in this way in preaching, the clear message is sent that the actual verbal content of Scripture—"what it says" and "what is in it"—is foundational to the church's life and ministry and not to be taken lightly.

More important, this kind of encoding sends the message that

---

7. See, for instance, Ernest Best, *From Text to Sermon: Responsible Use of the New Testament in Preaching* (Atlanta: John Knox Press, 1978).

Scripture is accessible, communicative, relevant, and approachable by everyone. The Bible is presented as a book that belongs to the community. It requires no experts in exegesis to unveil its meaning.

A translational encoding of Scripture promotes a *mimetic* form of anamnesis in the church. Translation promotes sacred remembrance as a form of imitation. Other signs of this mimetic intertext of anamnesis may be found throughout the life of the community—in the way people dress and act at church, in the language people use to address each other, in the kinds of Bible studies that exist in the church, and so on. At the heart of the community's remembering of its foundational events is imitation of those events in some way. The way that we are to make the past present today is to become an equivalent community.

In its narrowest, literalist sense, the community's anamnesis becomes a pale attempt to imitate or mimic precisely and literally in strange mythic gestures the manifest content of biblical life and forms of thought. In its dynamic equivalentist sense, the community's anamnesis becomes an attempt to imitate metaphorically or reflect (bend back or bend anew) the manifest content of biblical life and forms of thought. In its paraphrastic sense, the community's anamnesis becomes a truncated, diffused imitation that is more *in*flection (bent in, nuanced) than *re*flection.

NEGOTIATING A HEARING

In most cases, translation needs no negotiation to be heard and appreciated by those gathered to hear preaching, especially in Protestant denominations where Bible study groups have supported this kind of equivalentist hermeneutic for many years and where the perspicuity of Scripture is a fundamental principle of the Christian faith.

In many churches, however, the use of historical-critical methods of interpretation from the pulpit and in church school Bible study has introduced a certain amount of caution regarding the use of overly simplistic kinds of translation. As we will note in the next section of this chapter on the transitional interpretation of Scripture, many churches today have an ethos that no longer supports a full-fledged translational hermeneutic. Translation has to be revised and used in relation to other models of interpretation in order to be acceptable. At the end of the next section we will point out how to use translational and transitional styles of encoding Scripture back to back. The most important thing to do in such cases is to encode a demonstrable compatibility of interest between the two styles such that one style leads to and supports the other.

Although we could argue that translational churches need other methods of interpretation to keep translation from becoming non-critically paraphrastic, we could also argue that the recovery of a strong, critical, dynamic equivalentist form of translation is much needed in churches where the Bible has been removed from the laity by the narrow use of historical-critical methods. In other words, people in the pews need to hear interpretations that are not so arcane and subtle as to require a resident expert to draw them out. We will keep this need in mind as we examine the other styles of encoding Scripture and how their relationship to translation can be made compatible.

Transition (Traduction)

Transition means literally to "pass over." The second way that the scriptural code is styled in sermons is transitional. Scripture is encoded transitionally as an ancient puzzle that the sermon tries to solve in order that its hidden meaning can be passed over into the present. Scripture is fundamentally inaccessible and sphinxlike. It requires a special interpreter, a hermeticist (a go-between), to unpack its meaning and help the layperson make the transition from the past into the present.

Such an encoding of Scripture sometimes contains hints of suspicion at the naivete of translational approaches, which lack an appropriate consideration of the distance between the first century and today, and the need for special kinds of analysis of the original documents. Fackre points out that academically the transitionist sometimes separates hermeneutics from exegesis in order to emphasize the need to take into careful consideration the distance between the ancient culture and the modern context and the accompanying need for a special kind of interpreter or interpretation process to span the distance.[8]

8. Fackre, *The Christian Story,* 246.

Often a sense of a struggle to get at the meaning of the text is encoded in the preaching event. The congregation is made aware of ambiguities in the Scripture and cultural discrepancies. The manifest content of the text is abandoned in favor of less obvious, "deeper," or "original" meanings. These meanings are hard-won and thus sometimes wear the badge of insight in the language of preaching. As Fackre notes, the text "is often treated in a symbolist fashion as evocative of sensibilities otherwise untouched, or expressive of realities otherwise inaccessible."[9] Dynamic equivalencies, when drawn, are drawn at a deeper, more obscure level of textual analysis, are usually made more universal and open-ended, and are applied to deep historical, social, and cultural coordinates in today's world rather than to equivalent surface dimensions of life.

Most important in this struggle for insight is the effect of the process of historical-critical analysis. Often, the sermon encodes a sense of "the hard slogging work of finding out 'what it meant' in the obscurities of the past."[10] What is "behind the text" rather than "what the text says" is encoded as most important in the sermon.

If the Mary and Martha story is preached, the transitionist may note the social and religious iconoclasm in the ancient setting of a woman being taught by a rabbi, especially in her own home. On hearing this observation, the congregation knows that this insight is not immediately accessible on the surface of the text. It clearly represents the hermeticist's search on behalf of the community for the inaccessible meaning that resides "behind the text."

The traductional ("to lead across") variation of this transitional kind of scriptural encoding simply leans more on the authorial-communal axis of the search for the hidden meaning of the text. In Fackre's words, " 'whose is it' rather than 'what it meant' is the uppermost issue."[11] The meaning of the biblical text encoded in the sermon resides in the recovery of the "way in which interest shapes"[12] the biblical text. The scriptural code focuses, in the words

9. Ibid.
10. Ibid.
11. Ibid.
12. Ibid.

of E. D. Hirsh, on the "intention" of the author as the clue to the meaning of the biblical text.[13]

Again, in preaching the Mary and Martha story, the congregation may be invited to consider that Luke's Gospel does not mention the place (Bethany?) where this event took place. This (the preacher knows) is part of Luke's evangelical intention and is typical of the way he communicates that intention. The significance of this intention for today is encoded in the sermon with the statement: "In other words, *Luke is saying* that this (home visit from Jesus) could happen anywhere! This could happen to you!"[14]

CONSIDERATIONS

The transitional or traductional encoding of Scripture in preaching bears with it its own set of problems. First of all, it is in great danger of communicating more struggle than insight. For many people, once historical distance is experienced deeply, the problems of getting from then to now are overwhelming and can block any sense of relationship between Scripture and present experience.

Another problem, as I have already suggested, is the undercurrent communication of the message that Scripture is inaccessible to the laity without a hermeticist or group of go-betweens to dig behind the text for its true meaning. This message can promote both an elite within the church and corresponding distrust by laity of their own ability to read, study, and discuss Scripture without the presence of an expert. Transitionists and traductionists should be aware of the reductionist tendencies in their method of encoding Scripture in preaching, a reductionism that "reduces the meaning of a text to its critical component only, ignoring the common and canonical features."[15]

The transitional or traductional scriptural style is similar to the

---

13. See E. D. Hirsh, Jr., *Validity in Interpretation* (New Haven: Yale University Press). This is an oversimplification of Fackre's category of traduction in order to lean its meaning on text-specific information. He also includes in traduction the way that the interest of the contemporary interpreter influences interpretation. My choice is to assume this influence is at work in all of the models.

14. Quoted from a sermon by Joanna Adams at the General Assembly of the Presbyterian Church USA in Minneapolis in 1986.

15. Fackre, *The Christian Story,* 247.

translational style in the way that it underscores the foundational relationship between Scripture and the contemporary life of the Christian community. The struggle for insight from this ancient book signifies that Scripture is important and that the community still derives much of the substance of its life together from the events to which its pages bear witness. As with the translational approach, congregations are likely to hear the actual words of Scripture and are invited once again to reflect on their meaning for the church today. Like translation, transition or traduction is still a text-centered way of encoding Scripture in preaching.

A transitional or traductional use of Scripture promotes *historical* anamnesis in the church. The church remembers the historical events and the meaning of those events in their original historical context. Because the manifest content of the text is not the only locus of the text's meaning, this approach dramatically opens the field of discovery regarding what the church is to remember and how it is to be remembered. We always have more to discover about the nature and meaning of the foundational events of the faith as they are recorded and expressed in Scripture. Deep, hidden, and as yet unmined truths latent in the scriptural text keep it ever alive and changing in its impact on the church. The mystery of faith, that "Christ has died, Christ has risen, Christ will come again," is not univocal in its meaning but, indeed, had many meanings in its original context and throughout its history of interpretation. The church remembers that it is part of a historical communion of saints that has changed and that continues to change. It acknowledges that its own historically conditioned tools of interpretation keep open to revision the question of the final meaning of biblical events and testimonies.

The possibility is always present that this sense of the open-endedness and historicity of biblical interpretation can obscure both the veracity and the meaning of the foundational events of the faith by promoting a sense of confusion and ambiguity in the intertext of anamnesis. Sermons can communicate the idea that the church is not at all sure what it is recalling when it remembers its sacred origins. The "mystery of faith" can easily become the "ambiguity of faith" or the "confusion of faith." The church's remembrance of its sacred origins can become cloudy and uncertain, perhaps losing the power to influence how the church thinks and acts.

NEGOTIATING A HEARING

A hearing has already been negotiated for this style of encoding Scripture in many mainstream liberal and moderate evangelical churches. As we have already noted, however, transition is easily misperceived as arcane and even obscurantist by those who strongly expect a translational approach and for whom anamnesis is strictly mimetic. The person who is listening for something fairly obvious, on the surface of the text, that can be imitated or reflected in some fashion in that person's own world of thought and experience will be put off if what is "perfectly clear" in the text is sidestepped for some "deeper" historical insight. This disgruntled response will be compounded when this deeper meaning is then struggled with rather than unilaterally and immediately grafted onto the contemporary church's profile.

In this situation, the preacher who wants to negotiate a hearing for these things that lie behind the text and who wants to promote a historical anamnesis will need to look for the compatible interests rather than the conflicting interests between a translational hermeneutic and a transitional hermeneutic. The preacher will need to look for equivalents on the surface of the text that lead to insights that are behind the text. A strategy in which the manifest content is perceived as a pathway to latent content rather than a roadblock to that content will provide a way of bringing a congregation into a new hearing of the biblical material and a new understanding of what the church's anamnesis can be.

The preacher might put together translational and transitional perspectives on Martha's distraction such that the first leads to the second:

> According to Luke, while Mary was sitting at Jesus' feet, Martha was busy serving dinner all by herself. She was distracted by the difficulty and isolation of her task. How can she ever get things ready without some help?
>
> Maybe there was more to her distraction than this. After all, a rabbi never entered a house where a woman lived alone. Much less two women! And besides that, a rabbi was forbidden to teach the Torah to a woman. Could these things have compounded Martha's worries? On top of worrying about preparing dinner, could she also be worried

about the fact that this whole dinner violated rabbinic law and social custom?

This negotiating gesture appreciates the manifest content of the biblical story and locates a possible compatibility of interest between the manifest content and the historical-critical content. The translationists in the congregation are brought on board and are then invited to move via a compatible interest to the historical-critical level of interaction with the text. Rather than opposing the two levels of hearing Scripture or tacitly denying the existence of the former level of hearing, the two are brought into relationship with each other and found to be mutually supportive.

Meanwhile, the equivalentist impulse is honored as the congregation is invited to consider surface distractions in their own lives, even though they will now have to refine that simple equivalency in relation to our new "hard-won insight" about the distracting social and religious iconoclasm of Jesus. The preacher is still drawing out equivalencies, but now they are more open-ended, less mimetic, and more provocative, suggesting social and historical dimensions of the meaning of the text *at the same time* that they acknowledge the more obvious personal and devotional dimensions of the meaning of the text.

Transposition

A third text-centered style of encoding Scripture in preaching is transposition. Taken from the theory of music, the word *transposition* means "to have the same structure, yet in a different key." I have added this category to Gabriel Fackre's list because he subsumes some of its dynamics under the next category that we will consider, which Fackre calls *transformation*. Transposition is the text-centered side of transformation. Transformation, as we will see, is more concerned ultimately with the claim that the text makes upon its audience than with the exigencies of textual analysis. The dynamics of transposition, however, because of their powerful current impact on homiletics, need to be separated out and investigated in their own right.

In the transpositional style, Scripture is encoded as the rhetorical model for preaching. In essence, the sermon strives in some way to do rhetorically what the Scripture does or "intends" rhetorically. The sermon is not as concerned with either the commonsense meaning of the text or with meaning that lies behind the text. It is concerned with what is in front of the text, with how the language of the text functions. Instead of mining a meaning from the manifest content of Scripture or from somewhere behind the text and then communicating that meaning via any number of rhetorical strategies, the preacher tries to take from the scriptural text a rhetorical strategy for preaching. The sermon reflects the meanings in and behind the text but is most concerned with its form, that is, its model of communication.

This approach to the encoding of Scripture in preaching is currently the most popular new trend in homiletics.[16] Many consider it to be a more thoroughly biblical approach to preaching than other models because of its appropriation of the meaning of the biblical text in close relation to its rhetorical form. In the words of Leander Keck, the sermon should "impart a Bible-shaped word in a Bible-like way."[17]

Essentially, for the transpositionist, neither a timeless analogy of manifest content (translation approach) nor a time-bound correspondence of latent meaning (transition or traduction approach) is the heart of the church's relationship to Scripture. It is, rather, an analogy or similarity of "Christian consciousness."[18] This similarity is ultimately a similarity of language and form of expression (because all human consciousness is constituted by language).[19] Sermons, then, "replot plots" and "reintend intentional language."[20] When this happens, sermons encode a similar structure of faith consciousness as that found in Scripture, even though the meaning content for that structure may have changed. Rather than translating an

---

16. For the most helpful method for doing this, see David Buttrick, "Interpretation and Preaching," *Interpretation* (January 1981): 46–58. See also Don Wardlaw, ed., *Preaching Biblically: Sermons in the Shape of Scripture* (Philadelphia: Westminster Press, 1983); David Buttrick, *Homiletic: Moves and Structures* (Philadelphia: Fortress Press, 1987); and Richard L. Esslinger, *A New Hearing: Living Options in Homiletical Method* (Nashville: Abingdon Press, 1987).

17. Leander E. Keck, *The Bible in the Pulpit: The Renewal of Biblical Preaching* (Nashville: Abingdon Press, 1978), 106.

18. Buttrick, *Homiletic*, 269.

19. Ibid., 7.

20. Ibid., 301.

original or deciphering a puzzle, the sermon transposes a model of consciousness.

For instance, in the Mary and Martha passage one literary and rhetorical device within the text is the hidden negative. The rhetoric of the text conspires to conceal the *hamartia* or "sin" of Martha. We know that something is wrong, that she is not choosing the "good portion that shall not be taken away." However, the language of the text provides few clues as to what this *hamartia* might be. Indeed, the text presents Martha as the one who is doing what she ought to be doing, preparing dinner (and with no help from her sister).

The rhetorical strategy for preaching today can be determined by this linguistic intention. The sermon will be designed to replot this same hidden negative so that its structure is transposed into the faith consciousness of the contemporary church. The sermon is much more concerned to bother and provoke the congregation with this hidden negative than it is to pursue one idea, such as "the faith that cannot be taken away," or to unpack Luke's evangelical strategy in his own ecclesiastical and historical situation and attempt to make it relevant.

CONSIDERATIONS

The principal problem with transposition is that it tends to avoid encoding any factual or historical referent for the language of Scripture. Congregations hear stories and plots along with the intentions they express but are not invited to consider the veracity and meaning of what actually happened during Jesus' ministry. The good news is not what happened or even the early church's understanding of the meaning of what happened, but the way the biblical text "calls readers to interact with it, with life, and with their own world."[21] We might be so bold as to say that "new creation" is not so much communicated by this rhetorical negotiation as "new consciousness." The reference for this new consciousness is, in the words of R. A. Culpepper, "his story," not history.[22]

In practice, most of the usual things that rhetorically signify the deeper aspects of the text (such as its cultural and social references,

21. R. A. Culpepper, *Anatomy of the Fourth Gospel* (Philadelphia: Fortress Press, 1983), 236–37.
22. Ibid., 237.

facticity, historicity, and original meaning) are not given voice rhetorically in this kind of preaching because principally the language of the text and its performative function are what is essential for the sermon. What is behind the text, its life world, and the intentions of the author are "secondary" to the "primary" intentions of the text, which are embedded in the language of the text itself.[23]

Under the pressures of weekly preaching, the preacher who has learned to discern the rhetorical strategy and basic theological "field of concern"[24] of the language of a biblical text may, perhaps, decide to forgo any historical-critical, source, form, or redactional analysis of the text and thus reinforce the seeming naivete of this approach. Even when these critical gestures have been made, they may still fail to find any significant rhetorical voicing in the sermon because of the preacher's concentration on the plot and intention of the text's language and the conviction that mixing kinds and levels of scriptural interpretation in the sermon would be unfruitful.

Another problem is that transposition, like transition or traduction, is hermeticist in nature. It requires certain analytical skills that are not readily available to everyone. Some transpositionalist approaches to the biblical text can seem so hermetic as to be obscurantist.[25] Nevertheless, some scholars are working hard at making these approaches accessible, at least to the clergy.[26]

In spite of its problems, the transpositional encoding of Scripture does have the immediate advantage that it is text-centered. It is a style in which preaching is closely related to the specifics of particular texts themselves. This encoding sends the clear message, once again, that Scripture is foundational to the life of the church today. The congregation will hear the actual words of Scripture and interact

23. Buttrick, *Homiletic,* 300.
24. Buttrick, "Interpretation and Preaching," 52–53.
25. Tremper Longman III, *Literary Approaches to Biblical Interpretation* (Grand Rapids: Zondervan, 1987), 49. Longman is not alone in this observation, especially as it applies to structuralist and deconstructionist approaches. There is general unrest among biblical scholars about the "in language" of these schools of thought and the general unreadability and inaccessibility of their procedures to the layperson.
26. Thomas G. Long, *Preaching and the Literary Forms of the Bible* (Philadelphia: Fortress Press, 1989); Robert Alter, *The Art of Biblical Narrative* (New York: Basic Books, 1981) and *The Art of Biblical Poetry* (New York: Basic Books, 1985); and J. Kugel, *The Idea of Biblical Poetry* (New Haven: Yale University Press, 1981).

with the characters and ideas in the language of the text. This encoding sends a clear rhetorical signal that Scripture authorizes the life and witness of the Christian community.

The transpositional style of encoding Scripture promotes in the church a form of remembrance (anamnesis) that is centered in achieving rhetorical synchronicity between the expressive life of the ancient communities of faith and the expressive life of the church today. The church actually recalls the foundational events of the faith in the same way and for the same purposes as did the people of Israel and the early church.

Transposition supports in the church a *representational* intertext of anamnesis. Representation is an important part of the total meaning of anamnesis, and in essence what this kind of scriptural encoding does is represents or reperforms the scriptural text. As it does this, contemporary anamnesis (the recalling that is done in the church today) is synchronized or brought into a close structural and rhetorical relationship with its earliest types. The church appropriates actual forms of consciousness from its early history, some of which have names—parable, lament, doxology, and paranesis, for example—and many of which, like the hidden negative, do not have names because they are simply smaller rhetorical figures embedded in larger literary forms.

A potential problem is that a transpositional encoding of Scripture will promote archaism and irrelevance in the church's recalling of its foundational events. Re-presenting the form and formal intention of ancient literary genres can yield a flat, irrelevant rhetoric in the contemporary church. This effect is, of course, not necessarily the case where these forms and intentions are reframed and reenergized, but the tendency is to forget that forms of communication and linguistic intentions change over time and that the gospel has new ways and new purposes in today's world.

This kind of preaching also carries the danger of dissociating the church's recalling from the objects of its recall: the actual events and event communities that are foundational to the Christian faith. Then the "intertext of anamnesis" becomes an "intertext of textuality," and what is recalled is limited to a way of recalling and the world-in-consciousness that it intends. The language of recall cannot get beyond itself, and the church is left only with textuality or "intra-textuality": the Scripture text and its representational anamnetic intertext.[27]

Academic theorists of this method of literary and biblical inter-pretation are aware of this problem. Some believe that "textuality" cannot be escaped; this fact must be accepted, like the Fall, because of the limited nature of human language and expression.[28] For others, metaphor and symbol offer referential touchstones that keep this way of recalling rooted in referents that are transcendent to lan-guage.[29] For at least one scholar, textuality is the cause for rejoicing in the multiplicity of meanings in the biblical text and for "playing" with the text and its many meanings in new and imaginative ways.[30] For still others, this textuality will, perhaps, signify the solipsistic and atheistic end point of this kind of approach to Scripture and its ulti-mate bankruptcy for any religious tradition that relates revelation closely with a particular text.

Whatever the inherent problems are with this relatively new way of encoding Scripture, it does have the distinct advantage of putting the church in touch with its original ways of recalling. In essence, it recalls the early church's recall and makes it part of the church's anamnesis.

NEGOTIATING A HEARING

The novelty of the transpositional style of encoding Scripture means that observing it as a full-blown rhetorical style in the contemporary

27. I believe that this term was created by George Lindbeck in *The Nature of Doctrine: Religion and Theology in a Postliberal Age* (Philadelphia: Westminster Press, 1984) to describe what Hans Frei calls *figuration* in *The Eclipse of Biblical Narrative: A Study in Eighteenth and Nineteenth Century Hermeneutics* (New Haven: Yale Uni-versity Press, 1974), 3. The term refers to a way of "reinterpreting the world according to the patterns of . . . prior Scripture reading," which amounts to a "scriptural rein-scription of the world." David Dawson, "Allegorical Intertextuality in Bunyan and Winstanley," *The Journal of Religion* 70 (April 1990): 189.

28. Michael Edwards, *Towards a Christian Poetics* (London: Macmillan & Co., 1984).

29. See Buttrick, *Homiletic*; Paul Ricoeur, *Interpretation Theory: Discourse and the Surplus of Meaning* (Fort Worth: Texas Christian University Press, 1976); and Maurice Merleau-Ponty, *Consciousness and the Acquisition of Language* (Evanston, Ill.: North-western University Press, 1973); Philip Wheelwright, *Metaphor and Reality* (Bloom-ington: Indiana University Press, 1962); and Sallie McFague, *Metaphorical Theology: Models of God in Religious Language* (Philadelphia: Fortress Press, 1982).

30. John Dominic Crossan, *Cliffs of Falls: Paradox and Polyvalence in the Parables of Jesus* (New York: Seabury Press, 1980).

church is still difficult. Much of it exists in theory and in fledgling practice and has not yet borne the test of time. Because transposition is not yet an established rhetorical style in the church at large, its hermeticism, as we have already noted, may be misperceived.

By those used to a translational style, transposition may be misperceived and identified with translation itself because it seems to accept at face value the manifest content of the biblical text without probing its empirical, historical, and redactional underpinnings.

By those used to a transitional style, transposition may be perceived as naive and uncritical. For many in the pews on Sunday morning, especially those educated in the empirical sciences or medicine, it may seem to be a rhetoric of nonsense and naivete. Such preaching is easily misperceived as a commonsensical approach to the biblical text because it seems to encode only a relationship to what is on the surface of the biblical text (that is, its language). This impact is certainly not the intention of those who espouse this approach; for them, in many cases, the deep structure of the text is what is most important for preaching.

For instance, in a sermon on the narrative of Sarah and Abraham as recorded in Genesis 18:1-15, the transpositionist may be fascinated with the structural association between Sarah's laughter and the revelation of the identity of the three visitors who have visited the tent of Abraham in the heat of the day. The way the language works seems to be a literary twist that works to resolve the plot by disclosing the human correspondence (laughter is irony? doubt? joy?) to the unexpected and sometimes awkward ways of God.[31] This encoding is all very well, but the person listening for a transitional style is disturbed that the pregnancy of a ninety-year-old woman was left unsorted by the sermon; the translational listener is happy that the "facts" of the text have been left untampered with but has missed the point and goes away with the conviction that "sometimes you just have to laugh."

Some effort is required if the translationist and the transitionist are to be brought along. The preacher needs to find ways to bring

---

31. See Sue Ann Steffey's sermon "The Stuff That Covenant Is Made Of," in *Women and the Word: Sermons,* ed. Helen Gray Crotwell (Philadelphia: Fortress Press, 1978), 17–21.

the hearers to a new way of hearing the biblical text. This can be done only if the ways that people are expecting to hear are appreciated and used rather than shunned or avoided. Again, the clue is to search for compatible interests between the different styles.

The translational listener may be helped to hear a dynamic equivalence drawn between the unexpectedness of Sarah's situation and the surprising, awkward, and sometimes unexpected ways that God acts in our lives today. This comparison would provide a pathway into the unexpectedness of such events, given our medical and scientific assumptions today, and permit the transitionist to consider the ambiguity surrounding the grounding of such events both then and now. The preacher might then suggest that the language of the story does not focus on proving that God can and does intervene in the course of nature and history but rather on the strange response (laughter) that word of such intervention evokes after long years of waiting and watching. From there, the preacher can move to treat Sarah's laughter and catch up the congregation into the equivocal rhetorical impact it brings into the denouement of the story.

This same end can be accomplished in any number of other ways so that a different hearing is clearly distinguished from, but in close relation to, other expected hearings. No matter how or when in each sermon it is done, this kind of rhetorical gesture needs to be made if transpositional preaching and its accompanying representational anamnesis are going to win their own hearing in the church.

Transformation

The word *transformation* means to "change in form." In the transformational style, Scripture is encoded in preaching as "an active agent transforming the context into which it speaks."[32] In essence, it is encoded as gospel, the good news. Rather than binding Scripture to what can be mined from an analogical, historical, or literary analysis of the text and thus to the craft and perspective of the interpreter, Scripture has the power to disrupt, shatter, and transform the results of all of these interpretations in its role as active agent. In its purest theological conception, in the work of Karl Barth, Scripture rises out

---

32. Fackre, *The Christian Story,* 248.

of the ashes of critical analysis, transcends all contextual analogies and conceptualizations, and confronts or encounters the congregation and preacher as the Word of God.

Fackre notes the alliance of this style with the several traditions that take seriously the "internal testimony of the Holy Spirit" including "John Calvin and his heirs, the devotional encounter with Scripture in pieties and spiritualities, ancient and modern, the 'subjectivity' accents of Kierkegaard from which Barth himself learned so much, down to the 'word events' of the new hermeneutic, the disclosive and transformative accents of the symbolists and narrative theologies."[33] What is encoded in all of these traditions is the idea that someone is between the lines of the biblical text over "whom we have no control [who] enters our field of vision and our range of hearing" when we approach Holy Scripture in reverence and spiritual openness.[34]

By avoiding propositional meanings in or behind the text and by dodging concrete applications or equivalencies between such meanings and the contemporary context, the transformationist encodes a strong sense that the biblical text does not belong to anyone, not even the church. It is independent, free, and not ownable. We do not claim it or its meaning; it makes a claim on us.[35] Its story is wholly other and can never be adequately translated, understood, or represented in any context.

The transformational style encodes a much stronger affective element than do the first three styles. Scripture is an evocative agent. Its role is various: to make a claim on, to encounter, to confront, to shake, to inbreak, to erupt, to disrupt, and to disclose.[36] The text brings with it an encounter with the truth of oneself and the truth of God. In a more Bultmannian mode, the text is the bearer of a crisis that demands a decision and reorientation of human existence.

33. Ibid.
34. Ibid.
35. Thomas G. Long, "Shaping Sermons by Plotting the Text's Claim upon Us," in Wardlaw, *Preaching Biblically,* 84–100; *The Witness of Preaching* (Louisville: Westminster/John Knox Press, 1989), 77; and *Preaching and Literary Forms,* 33–34. Although he accents the wedding of transposition and transformation, Long seems to desire that the preacher unite transitional, transpositional, and transformational styles by integrating the transformational concern of "discerning the claim that text makes upon the current life of the community of faith" into the exegetical process at its very end.
36. Fackre, *The Christian Story,* 249.

The text bears witness to something disruptive that, in the words of J. J. von Allmen, "strikes the church from the outside"[37] and continually shakes its very foundations and alters its most hallowed presuppositions.

CONSIDERATIONS

One of the great strengths of the transformational encoding of Scripture is that it heightens the church's awareness of the "sovereign subject matter" of Scripture.[38] This sovereign subject matter is not the objective facts, historical truths, or "ways of intending" of the text, but the Subject about whom the text is written, namely, Jesus Christ, crucified, resurrected, and laying claim to human lives. Because this Subject is always sovereign to the church, the church is challenged to be constantly aware of the limitations of its interpretations and the provisionality of its institutional life.

One problem with transformation is that in its concern for the proclamation of the good news it may cease to express any concern for the historicity of the foundational events of faith. At this point transformation, as we have already noted, is the forerunner of transposition. The concern with the "Word-event" and with the powerful expressive impact of the gospel in the church can obscure concern with the historical events behind the text to which the text refers. Like transposition, this ahistoricism can be misperceived as hermeneutical naivete unless the kind of rhetorical style through which preacher and congregation are communicating is negotiated carefully.

Although transformation gave birth to transposition, transformation is not always as clearly a text-centered rhetorical style in the church as is transposition. Although the particularities of the text remain important to the sermon in some models of transformational preaching, clearly the sovereign subject matter of the text and its claim upon human life predominate and control the rhetoric of the

37. J. J. von Allmen, *Worship: Its Theology and Practice* (New York: Oxford University Press, 1965), 143–44.
38. Thomas E. Provence, "The Sovereign Subject Matter: Hermeneutics in the *Church Dogmatics*," in *A Guide to Contemporary Hermeneutics: Major Trends in Biblical Interpretation,* ed. Donald K. McKim (Grand Rapids: Wm. B. Eerdmans, 1986), 241–62.

scriptural code in the sermon. The biblical text is still absolutely central and necessary because no knowledge of this subject matter exists apart from the Bible.[39] Ultimately, Scripture is, however, the midwife to a convictional relationship with Jesus Christ.

As we have noted, the true transformationist is wary of any hard-and-fast attempt to determine messages or meanings in or behind the biblical text or to apply them directly to the modern context. Transformationists will use translation and transition but are ultimately suspicious of them in the pulpit. How transposition was spawned from this transformational model is easy to see because the concern with the how of the text allows a focus on evocative effect and symbolic power in preaching while precluding final decisions about particular meanings that the text might have, either in its original context or today. The transformationist tries to avoid any direct application of the text to the contemporary context. Texts are usually related to paradigmatic people and situations, not to specific people and events. The Spirit (or perhaps our inductive reason) is to be ultimately in charge of the process of "speaking a special word to our condition."[40] Our job is simply to help the text to speak, to give voice to its voice in such a way as to call forth a yes or no response.

The transformationist is seldom concerned with the whole biblical text or pericope, for the whole of a text seldom addresses the preacher's congregation with evocative power. Tom Long, who wants preachers to learn to combine especially transition, transposition, and transformation, notes that "the preacher's task . . . is not to replicate the text but to *regenerate* the impact of *some portion* of that text."[41] A less text-centered transformationist would change this statement slightly and say that the preacher wants to *generate* an impact (encounter, crisis, claim) by focusing the congregation's attention on some portion of the text.[42]

In preaching the Mary and Martha text from Luke's Gospel, the

---

39. Likewise (at least in Barth's argument), there is no true understanding of the Bible apart from acquaintance with the subject matter of the Bible, Jesus Christ. Provence, "Sovereign Subject Matter," 252.

40. Fackre, *The Christian Story*, 248.

41. Long, *Preaching and Literary Forms*, 33.

42. In my thinking, a good contemporary example of this kind of preaching is that of William Sloane Coffin, Jr., formerly of Riverside Church in New York City.

transformationist might single out the disruption that Mary's actions caused in the household, the same kind of disruption that bold, solicitous responses to Jesus Christ always cause to those for whom order, manners, and law are paramount. The sermon would go in search of ways to make the congregation experience the disruptive power of such bold responses to Christ in order to bring the impact of that portion of the text alive in the congregation's hearing.

The transformationist style promotes a *kerygmatic* intertext of anamnesis in the church. It keeps the church's anamnesis in close touch with the kerygma, the proclamation of the scandalous claims of the cross and resurrection of Jesus Christ and the call to repentance, to a yes or no stance in relation to those claims. The foundational events of the faith are recalled in preaching through the prism of this kerygma or, in the words of David Buttrick, from the "symbolic-reflective" stance of being "in Christ."[43] Thus, as has been noted, the community recalls the foundational events of faith not as "facts," "history," or "his-story," but as "gospel."[44] The kind of recall that is promoted in the church is not mimetic, historic, or textualist; it is kerygmatic recall. The church recalls the radical claims of the gospel and the claims that that gospel makes on its hearers. It is an energized, performative form of recall, one that seeks encounter, decision, and transformation as the way the foundational events of the faith are brought to life in the church today.

NEGOTIATING A HEARING

The principal problems that arise when negotiating a hearing for the transformational style is its often emotional, evocative nature and the sometimes narrow (or nonexistent) focus of its hermeneutical interest. For those who are listening for the whole text to be broken into helpful dynamic applications for daily life (translation) or who are concerned that the deep meaning of the text be found and struggled with in relation to contemporary experience (transition), the text may seem to be merely a pretext for the preacher's transformational agenda. Listeners may complain that they are swayed more by the conviction and seeming authenticity of the preacher than they

---

43. Buttrick, *Homiletic,* 13–15.
44. Ibid., 15.

are by any precise claims that the foundational events of the faith may actually make upon their own lives. This impression is left especially if the critical analysis of the biblical text is left undone or only partly done because ultimately the gospel is what is being preached. The parody of this approach is the preacher who prepares nothing because he or she wants to be "under the Spirit" when preaching. The preacher knows that he or she can find the "gospel" in any text—so why study the text?

Quite often, when this happens, the good news is reduced to its broadest terms, and all texts are preached identically; no matter what the biblical text, the message seems to be the same. The multifaceted aspects of the kerygma and the breadth and depth of its claims may be left unvoiced. It presents the clear danger of a kind of redundancy that will close the intertext of anamnesis and make it strictly memorialist, an erected tombstone commemorating past events in only one way. This closure is possible whether the preacher reads the good news evangelistically, existentially, socially, or in whatever way.

One way to overcome this proclivity, it seems, is to keep alive some search for the particular meaning(s) of the text in preaching, either through translation or transition. This approach acknowledges that the claims of the gospel are not simply affective hot air or rhetorical evocation but that those claims come "through, not around the objective truth claims made by that text."[45] It keeps the congregation attentive to the multiplicity of claims upon human life that the gospel had in its early contexts and, we presume, still has in ours. It also highlights compatibilities of interest between different styles of hearing in a way that brings on board those who are used to other ways of hearing the Scripture.

Fackre rightly observes that the backlash by early neoorthodox theologians and more recently by symbolists against "propositional interpretations" may lead to a "reduction of cognition to affective evocation."[46] Nevertheless, the transformational style is correct in showing that, having discovered the truth claims of the biblical text, we must not leave them like the "assertions dissected in the classrooms of logic" but enable them to "reach us at the level of deep

45. Fackre, *The Christian Story,* 249.
46. Ibid.

affect and make a personal claim upon us."[47] For this reason, the transformational style, if properly negotiated, can bring much in the way of life and dynamism to the church's anamnesis.

Trajection

Trajection is the act of "casting or throwing across." The trajectional encoding of Scripture is context-centered. It encodes the idea that the biblical text has an inner meaning, a "purpose of God" that is always developing further implications and meanings (its s*ensus plenior*) as it is interpreted in different epochs and locales.[48] This "fuller sense of the meaning is in continuity with the original trajectory"[49] in the biblical text. This trajectory has simply cast its inner meaning forward into a new context and location for interpretation.

Whereas the translationist starts with the language about the original events testified to in Scripture and then searches for equivalencies in the new context, the trajectionist starts with the cultural context in which the church finds itself today and asks how that context might "press the Christian community to examine its texts in a new light."[50] The new context in which the church finds itself becomes a catalyst for the discovery of new implications for trajectories of meaning within the biblical text. The horizons of meaning that the biblical text opens for the church are open horizons. From this perspective, biblical revelation is trajective: it is "cast or thrown across" time and awaits new occasions for its fullness to be manifested and understood.

Examples of trajection abound. New implications of Paul's statements regarding salvation by grace through faith awaited the epoch of the Reformation. Similarly, new implications of Paul's statements regarding the "slave" and "free" awaited the period of the American Civil War to be understood. Today, trajectories regarding the role and image of women in the Bible are beginning to have new implications because liberation and feminist theologians have invited the church to examine the biblical texts in a new light.

We can easily argue that keeping these contextual exigencies from

47. Ibid.
48. Ibid., 250.
49. Ibid.
50. Ibid., 251.

influencing the scriptural code is impossible, no matter what style is predominant. The pastoral, ideological, social, political, and personal commitments of both the church and the preacher enter into any encoding of Scripture. We saw this influence where the paraphrastic-translationist encoding of Scripture was present. For the trajectionist, however, the personal commitments of the preacher are not strictly catalysts for meaning; the cultural context within and beyond the church is the primary catalyst, and this contextual catalyst leads the scriptural code at every turn. The meaning of the biblical text will be presented as dependent upon this contextual catalyst, not simply as independent and supportive of personal issues or concerns.

CONSIDERATIONS

Whereas the transformationist is reluctant to contextualize the gospel because of the dangers of acculturation,[51] trajectionist preachers are constantly reexamining their own understanding of what the claims of the gospel are today (contextual hermeneutic) and altering that understanding periodically so that the congregation's perception of what the claims of the text are in the contemporary context will not become locked in and stereotypical. Such contextual reexamination sends the preacher back to the text to look for new claims and new meanings for older trajectories, as well as for new trajectories yet undiscovered.

Assume for the moment that I am a preacher with a trajectional style ministering in a low-income urban congregation made up of 70 percent women. Because I have studied Reinhold Niebuhr and Augustine, I may believe that sin is idolatrous pride and that God's grace is forgiveness that leads to humility and self-surrender. When I have finished my exegesis of the Mary and Martha text, I am drawn in by the hidden negative in the text. If there is a *hamartia* for Martha in this text, it surely is not pride! Is wanting to prepare a nice dinner for someone you love and honor prideful? Why do I sense something redemptive for my congregation in the actions of Mary? Certainly her insistence on listening to Jesus and her neglect of Martha show something more than self-surrender and humility.

51. Ibid., 249.

Rather than rethinking my exegesis, I begin to rethink what redemption looks like in my low-income congregation of mostly women. In this process of rethinking, I happen to read Judith Plaskow's *Sex, Sin and Grace* and Sue Dunfee's *Beyond Servanthood.*[52] I am struck by both authors' use of the idea of "hiding" or "the failure to turn toward self" in relation to the experience of sin by women and marginalized groups of people. The more I think about it, sin as hiding makes a great deal more sense in my context than sin as pride. Such a metaphor enables me to see grace more as forgiveness linked with freedom and empowerment than as forgiveness linked with self-abnegation and humility. When I return to the Mary and Martha text, my hunch that the text is redemptive in my context is confirmed. Jesus' entrance into the house and his actions there appear as acts of empowerment. They call forth new patterns of behavior and ways of being, while empowering choices for "the good portion that shall not be taken away." Mary's response to Jesus appears bold. It is clearly a "turning toward self" in the act of turning boldly toward the new realm of God that Jesus manifests. By revising my contextual hermeneutic, I have dramatically changed my understanding of the claim that the text makes upon the contemporary church. I see something now in the text that has awaited this particular historical and contextual moment for realization.

You might say that similar conclusions could have been reached by simply drawing out a dynamic equivalence between the historical-critical discovery of the iconoclasm of a rabbi teaching a woman and the contemporary situation of women in the church and world today. To some extent this comment is true. The translational and transitional styles, however, render this conclusion as something that, in Fackre's words, "has *application* for" a particular contemporary "setting." The trajectionist style renders this conclusion as something that "has *implication* for all settings."[53] The congregation hears their situation not as a particular location in which to find equivalencies

52. Judith Plaskow, *Sex, Sin and Grace: Women's Experience and the Theologies of Reinhold Niebuhr and Paul Tillich* (Lanham, Md.: University Press of America, 1980); and Susan Nelson Dunfee, *Beyond Servanthood: Christianity and the Liberation of Women* (Lanham, Md.: University Press of America, 1989).

53. Fackre, *The Christian Story,* 253.

for or insights about a specific biblical event but as part of an open-ended arena in which to begin to appropriate more of the implications of a whole biblical trajectory of meaning.

This style promotes a *heuristic* intertext of anamnesis. It is a recalling of the foundational events of the faith that is done through the discovery and interpretation of the ongoing implications of those events in the contemporary context. The congregation does not strive to imitate, understand, re-present, or stand within the claims of the foundational events of faith; they strive to discover those events and their meaning in their own midst. From a trajectional style in the pulpit, congregations learn that the contextual hunches, suspicions, yearnings, questions, and interests that they bring to biblical events are essential to how these events come to life in the community.

NEGOTIATING A HEARING

Again, the translationist, transitionist, transpositionist, and transformationist need to be brought along if they are going to be able to hear Scripture in this way. For all of them, at a surface glance trajectionism brings with it the problems that come with acculturation. Of course, the Bible is an acculturated text to begin with, a "new and blended pattern" resulting from "continuous transmission of traits and elements between diverse peoples," to paraphrase the dictionary definition of *acculturation,* and certainly acculturation is a part of any form of biblical interpretation.

Nevertheless, the trajectionist lets the new context *control* the interpretive process. The new context reopens the horizon of the text's meaning, which quite often results in a revision or change in both the original and traditional meanings of the text. Change can be perceived as an ideological truncation of the meaning of the text or as an attempt to harmonize text and context that dilutes the text's true meaning. This reaction is especially likely if new meanings are, at first glance, contradictory or very different from traditional or original meanings.

Our picture of the empowered Mary emerging from hiding to turn toward herself could be heard as a new and blended pattern that stands in contradiction to traditional meanings. It could easily seem to represent an ideological truncation of those meanings. To preach this new implication of the text out of the blue, with no attempt to relate these observations to other levels of textual hearing, would be to compound the problem. For the translationist, the preacher needs to go back into the text to revise surface equivalencies, perhaps focusing on the deepened sense of isolation and distance Martha feels amidst the old patterns of behavior due to Mary's actions ("my sister has left me . . . to serve alone"). We all feel this way when we see others strike out on their own and make it. For the transitionist, this could be related to the social and religious iconoclasm of Jesus that both empowers Mary and accentuates the tensive distance between Mary and Martha. For the transpositionist, the preacher might equate the text's hidden negative with the hiding that Martha continues to do in her anxious commitment to conventional roles. For the transformationist, the preacher might locate a new transformational moment in the narrative (what about "Martha, Martha"?) that shows Jesus attempting to turn Martha toward herself.

Of course, trying to bring everyone along at the same time may not be necessary. The important thing to do, as we have been suggesting all along, is to discern the principal styles of interpretation in your congregation and encode Scripture in such a way that those who represent these styles sense that their way of interpreting is being responded to at the same time that you are promoting another model.

The benefits of keeping trajection in a close relation to other styles of encoding Scripture do not stop here, however. When you relate the styles, you are enabling those who share your trajectional hermeneutic and heuristic form of anamnesis to hear more clearly and at more depth the authorizing source for the trajectory of meaning that they are discovering in their midst. The effect is one of making the text-to-context interaction a two-way street, and it keeps the results of the acculturation process from actually becoming either the diluted insights of a facile harmonization or the truncated insights of a fixed ideology.

APPLYING THE SCRIPTURAL CODE

We have now had a chance to examine briefly the content of the scriptural code and five ways that this code sponsors the church's anamnesis today. The first layer of our rhetorical schema looks like this:

Scriptural Code

Content: Direct or indirect allusions to Scripture or biblical events

Intertext: Anamnesis, the way in which the church recalls the foundational events of the faith in order to make them present in the community today

Styles: Code styles sponsor intertext styles (Table 3)

TABLE 3
Scriptural Code and Intertext Styles

Code Style	*Sponsors*	*Intertext Style*
Translation		Mimetic anamnesis
Transition (Traduction)		Historical anamnesis
Transposition		Representational anamnesis
Transformation		Kerygmatic anamnesis
Trajection		Heuristic anamnesis

In this chapter I have suggested that at the heart of what preaching means is the deep concern to bring the foundational events of the faith to life in the community of faith today. We have seen how this goal is accomplished in preaching through different ways of encoding Scripture. The first part of the rhetorical schema is designed to enable preachers to become more conscious about what they are saying and doing when they use Scripture in particular ways in preaching.

Let me now be prescriptive for a moment, set this first part of the schema into a broader analytical process, and indicate a strategy for strength in the encoding of Scripture in your preaching.

Homiletical Analysis

Begin the process with an analysis of what you are already doing with Scripture in your preaching. Using the schema as a guide, go back through at least four or five months of your sermons, and categorize your scriptural allusions according to the five *T*s. If you do not use a manuscript, you may want to tape your sermons for a few months and transcribe them so that you can study them more easily.

As you go through these sermons, you may note a mixture of these rhetorical styles at work in your preaching. However, one style or at most a mixture of two styles is probably central in your preaching. You will probably not find a regular mix of more than two of these styles. Take note of the dominant style or styles.

Congregational Analysis

The second step is to gain some knowledge of your congregation's basic approach to Scripture. It can be done informally, by participant observation at such things as Bible studies, in Christian education classes, and in conversation, or through the development of a direct questionnaire. Congregational study books and manuals are beginning to provide methods of congregational self-study that include this kind of component.[54] You may want to incorporate a Scripture-use profile as one portion of a larger congregational self-study. Again, no matter what process of analysis you use, your job is to take note of the predominant style or mixture of two styles that best characterizes your congregation's basic style of encoding Scripture.

Theological and Pastoral Analysis

The third step is to analyze theologically and pastorally what you are doing and determine what you want and need to do.

Theological Reflection

In order to help you begin your theological reflection, let me make a few suggestions regarding at least one theological underpinning for the Scripture code and anamnesis intertext: the theology of revelation. Each rhetorical style in the schema implies a different theology of revelation.

The preacher in one tradition may have a propositional view of revelation in which the revelation of God is embodied, according to Avery Dulles, "in propositional language so that it can make a definite claim on our assent."[55] This preacher will want to be aware that a translational style supports this presupposition. A preacher in

---

54. James F. Hopewell, *Congregation: Stories and Structures* (Philadelphia: Fortress Press, 1987).

55. Avery Dulles, "The Symbolic Structure of Revelation," *Theological Studies* 41 (March 1980): 52.

another tradition, however, may believe that words "can promise a revelation yet to be given: they can subsequently report what has been revealed through deeds; but they are not themselves revelation."[56] In this instance, the preacher will need to be aware that similarly, in the transitionist style, the meaning of revelation resides in history, not words about history. In another tradition, the preacher may hold fast to the belief that revelation is God's free act in Jesus Christ and that Jesus Christ "cannot be contained in history, even though [he] may touch history at a dimensionless point, as a tangent touches a circle."[57] The preacher will need to be aware that in the transformationist style revelation is likewise removed from both the realm of history and the realm of language. In yet another tradition, the preacher may understand revelation, in the words of Dulles, as "symbolic disclosure" in which "an externally perceived sign . . . works mysteriously upon the human consciousness so as to suggest more than it can clearly describe or define."[58] Biblical history is important, not as historical facts, but as "a narrative structure in social consciousness."[59] In this case, the preacher needs to be aware that in both transposition and trajection revelation is "symbolic disclosure." If, as a symbolist, the preacher determines that biblical structures should be the more significant theological element for the determination of the meaning of revelation, he or she will gravitate toward transpositional approaches. If, as a symbolist, the preacher determines that the broader symbolic life of social consciousness (symbols, myths, rituals, dramas, actions, paradigms of thought) is the more determinative element in the meaning of revelation, the preacher will want to move toward trajectional approaches.

Pastoral Reflection

As a pastor, you will need to reflect (preferably with members of your congregation) on your style, your congregation's style, and the theological issues raised by each style in relation to the life of faith.

---

56. Ibid., 53.
57. Ibid., 54.
58. Ibid., 56–57.
59. Buttrick, *Homiletic*, 116.

If your style and the congregation's style are similar or the same, you may begin by saying, "Fine, we're communicating, at least at this level of my preaching." Then ask some more strategic kinds of questions: Is this where we need to stay? Are there other ways of recalling the foundational events of the Christian faith that might be important or helpful from the pulpit? How can we be stronger and more intentional in this model that we share? Are there ways to better include those in our midst who do not share this dominant style?

If your style and the congregation's are different, you may want to ask a different set of questions: Are we consciously or unconsciously knocking heads? How compatible are our different styles? Do I need to appreciate the congregation's style more? Is it theologically and pastorally important to promote one of these styles or perhaps a completely different style? If my style is important to promote, what do I need to do to "negotiate a hearing" for it?

Conscious Commitment

The final step in your process is to commit yourself consciously to a particular way of encoding Scripture in preaching. This commitment should now be rooted in theological and pastoral decisions based on a clear understanding of both you and your congregation. This commitment will mean two things.

Hermeneutical Focus

First of all, your commitment will mean that you consciously accentuate a particular hermeneutical question when you are doing your biblical exegesis for preaching. Here are some representational questions for each style:

Translation

What is each biblical character, action, or idea in the language of the text like in the life of individuals, church, or world today?

Transition

What is the historical, social, authorial, and literary meaning of this text, and what significance does this have for today?

Transposition

What does the language of this text do? How does it "perform" (orient consciousness)?

Transformation

What within this text has the power to change lives in my audience, if it were really heard? What claim does this text make on my hearers?

Trajection

What hunches, suspicions, curiosities, and problems are sparked in my relationship with this text by my context in ministry and in the world? What do I see in my context that forces me to rethink or think carefully about something in this text?

You may be asking yourself all of these kinds of questions already as a part of your exegetical process. In my recipe this process is a must. It enables you to hear the text more completely in relation to your own context. It also will enable you to broaden ways of encoding the text and to negotiate better a hearing for your particular style. Accepting the fact that one or two styles will tend to dominate anyway, however, your job is to become conscious and strategic in your use of one style at this point and to focus your attention on one kind of hermeneutical question so that it will clearly become basic or foundational to your preaching. In other words, you will want to end your hermeneutical questioning with one of these questions and make that question pivotal in your preaching.

Rhetorical Focus

Second, you will need to pay attention to the rhetoric of your preaching to be sure that you are encoding Scripture in the style to which you are committed. You will need to be sure that this style is strongly present in your preaching (that it vouches) and that it is responsive to other styles in such a way that it leads toward the style to which you are committed (it negotiates and promotes).

Short of this entire process of self-analysis and congregational analysis in theological and pastoral perspective, you may simply want to take note of your style and learn to promote and negotiate its hearing in better and more strategic ways. At the very least, you may now see more clearly how you encode Scripture and what this sponsors in the life of your congregation.

2

THE SEMANTIC CODE

One way to think about the meaning of a sermon would be to analyze the meanings "in the people" involved. Such an analysis would investigate what the preacher means—what he or she intends to say—and then analyze what the sermon means to the congregation and what its effects are on various individuals or on a whole group of people. Intentional and affective meaning are sometimes called "psychological meaning,"[1] which is an extremely important dimension of meaning in preaching. Concern with this dimension of meaning keeps homileticians and preachers in close touch with interpersonal communication theory and with theories of public speaking that accentuate ways of promoting congruence between intentional and affective meaning.[2] In this chapter, however, we will focus attention on another dimension of meaning, *semantic meaning,* that is, meaning once it has been given over to language (encoded) in the context of a larger discourse. Our focus is on how meaning is rhetorically manifested in the language of sermons.

---

1. Paul Ricoeur, *Interpretation Theory: Discourse and the Surplus of Meaning* (Fort Worth: Texas Christian University Press, 1976), 13–14.
2. See, for instance, Myron Chartier, *Preaching as Communication: An Interpersonal Perspective* (Nashville: Abingdon Press, 1981); and Merrill R. Abbey, *Communication in Pulpit and Parish* (Philadelphia: Westminster Press, 1973).

CONTENT

The content of the semantic code is the meaning of the sermon or, more profoundly, it is the meaning of the gospel as it is encoded in the language of the sermon. The word *semantic* comes from the Greek word *sēmeion,* which means "sign." Semantics designates anything that has to do with meaning once it is given over to language or "signification." In other words, semantics is concerned with meaning in language, not with meaning "in people."[3]

One way to look at the content of the semantic code is to focus on the relationship between the words a preacher chooses and what they designate, between what some linguists call *signifiers* and their *signifieds.*[4] In the study of rhetoric and communication, however, word-meaning is only one part of discourse-meaning.[5] At the level of discourse, meaning exists not simply in individual words but, more importantly, in combinations of words—sentences, paragraphs, and communication events as a whole. The basic unit of meaning at the level of discourse is not the word but the sentence, and its subject-predicate structure is fundamental to how meaning is codified in sermons.[6]

3. David K. Berlo, *The Process of Communication: An Introduction to Theory and Practice* (New York: Holt, Rinehart & Winston, 1960), 184.

4. Ferdinand de Saussure, *Course in General Linguistics,* trans. Wade Baskin (New York: McGraw-Hill, 1966).

5. See Ricoeur, *Interpretation Theory,* 6–8; see also Michel Foucault, *The Archaeology of Knowledge and the Discourse on Language* (New York: Pantheon Books, 1972); Emile Benveniste, *Problémes de linguistique générale* (Paris: Gallimard, 1966); Julia Kristeva, *Desire in Language* (New York: Columbia University Press, 1980); Frederic Jameson, *The Political Unconscious: Narrative as a Socially Symbolic Act* (Ithaca, N.Y.: Cornell University Press, 1980); and Diane Macdonell, *Theories of Discourse: An Introduction* (New York: Blackwell, 1986).

6. In the late 1950s Grady Davis's book *Design for Preaching* (Philadelphia: Fortress Press, 1958) popularized the idea of the subject-predicate relationship as a key to preaching "complete thoughts" or "ideas." To have unity and completion of thought in sermons was to have sermons that could be capsulized in one sentence with a clear and creatively fashioned subject and predicate.

Joseph H. Danks has shown that an intimate connection exists between thought and language, between idea and linguistic formulation. On the basis of his research, he states that "the process of sentence construction is the same process as generating the idea (the thinking process itself), at least for those tasks in which a verbal response is required." In other words, the very "schema of the idea" has "its semantic representation in the sentence" ("Producing Ideas and Sentences," in *Sentence Production,* ed. S. Rosenberg [New York: John Wiley & Sons, 1977], 248–50).

Keeping this in mind, the first semantic content encoded in sermons are categories of thought and subjects. A *category of thought* is the broad subject area or "semantic domain"[7] within which a sermon is operating. *Subjects* are particular topics that a sermon is addressing within a semantic domain or category of thought. Table 4 provides some examples of basic homiletical categories of thought and the kinds of subjects that fall within each category.[8]

The second meaning-content encoded in sermons are *predicates,* that is, what is being said about those subjects—their qualities, classes, relationships, actions, and the like. People who listen to a sermon struggle to come away with a more or less complete sentence or string of complete sentences that says what the sermon was about. As they listen to our sermon on the Mary and Martha story, for instance, they listen for more than subjects like distraction, empowerment, or grace. They put together sentences such as "Distraction can lead to isolation," "Jesus Christ empowers us to come out of hiding," "Grace is an unconventional houseguest," and so on.

In *Building the Word: The Dynamics of Communication and Preaching*, J. Randall Nichols makes use of a provocative piece of research by George A. Miller[9] on "how people perceive and categorize their worlds."[10] On the basis of this research, Nichols points out that "virtually all people think in terms of seven separate categories (plus or minus two) about any one thing at any one time."[11] He goes on to suggest that no matter what biblical lectionary is being used, preachers still have a limited lectionary of ideas at any one time that they are using in their preaching.[12] Nichols creates an "idea inventory," which is a brief content analysis process that preachers can try if they want to discern their basic seven (plus or minus two)

7. See Eugene A. Nida, *Componential Analysis of Meaning: An Introduction to Semantic Structures* (The Hague: Mouton, 1979).

8. I have adapted these categories from William A. Christian, *Meaning and Truth in Religion* (Princeton: Princeton University Press, 1964), 169–84.

9. George A. Miller, "The Magic Number Seven, Plus or Minus Two," in *Language and Thought,* ed. Donald C. Hildum (Princeton: Van Nostrand, 1967), 3–32.

10. J. Randall Nichols, *Building the Word: The Dynamics of Communication and Preaching* (New York: Harper & Row, 1980), 52.

11. Ibid., 52.

12. Ibid., 56–57.

TABLE 4
Homiletical Categories and Subjects

Category	*Subjects*
1. *Qualities*	Wisdom, love, detachment, unity, empowerment, freedom, creativity, happiness
2. *Relations*	Nature and humanity, God and humanity, justice and freedom, being and becoming
3. *Natural entities*	The sun, the earth, light, the "land"
4. *Particular human individuals and groups*	Jesus, Martin Luther King, Jr., the church, this church (we, I, you), the dead, the Christian tradition, humanists, our neighborhood
5. *Nature*	The environment, creation, cosmos
6. *Humankind*	The self, all people (we), culture, society, "the world," history, perceptions, actions, emotions
7. *Pure forms*	Eternity, ideals, essences, the Truth, the Good, Evil, the Holy, grace
8. *Pure states*	Being, transcendence, becoming, spirit, "in Christ," nothingness
9. *Transcendent or "ground" active beings*	God, Satan, Christ, Holy Spirit, communion of saints, angels, demons

ideas for preaching. These ideas find their way, usually unconsciously, into the "semantic code" of the preacher's sermons. They are the lexicon of categories of thought, subjects, and predicates that each sermon assumes or anticipates.

In order to take a strategic, long-range approach to meaning, you will need to begin with an analysis of what you actually tend to preach about regularly (idea inventory). You will discern what the meaning of the gospel is in your preaching. Then you will move to a theological and pastoral analysis of what you want and need to preach about. Finally, you will raise the issue of how to accomplish this (communication skills). Once you determine what your preaching is usually about, then the issue of psychological congruence between these ideas, those you intend to communicate, and those your congregation actually hears can be addressed with more precision. Communication skills and techniques can be used more strategically to change, deepen, or reinforce aspects of that semantic lexicon rather than to ensure that your congregation "knows and remembers what I'm talking about this Sunday morning." We will return to this more strategic approach to semantic content at the end of this chapter.

One final word about the semantic content of sermons. We could argue that everything in a sermon "means" and therefore is potentially part of the semantic code. Certainly everything in a sermon means, but not everything in a sermon signifies meaning. Not everything in a sermon says "meaning is here," "here's what we're talking about," or "here's what we might be talking about." When you think about the content of the semantic code in sermons, then you must focus on phrases or statements that actually signify meaning. Anything in a sermon that (1) indicates that a category, subject, or predicate of sermon meaning exists; (2) says what a category subject or predicate is; or (3) suggests what a category, subject, or predicate might be is part of the content of the semantic code of that sermon.

INTERTEXT OF TRUTH

As we approach the question of the sermon's relationship to truth, Pilate's words "What is truth?" ring in our ears, and we are reminded that an answer to that question has already been given in Jesus Christ. The truth of Jesus Christ, however, is textualized (shaped in language) in different ways in different communities of discourse. Moreover, the truth of Jesus Christ is not the only truth that Christian congregations express, although it is usually central and pivotal. All kinds of things are held to be true by different congregations: "The devil is trying to get you," "The fundamentalists are taking over the world," "God is neither male nor female," "God loves the sinner but not the sin," and so on. We are not saying that these statements are uniformly accepted truth statements or that they ever make actual truth claims in the community. They may be hotly debated or only suggested. Such truth statements are simply the kinds of messages that help to shape what is held to be true in a congregation. What a congregation and preacher hold to be true for their community is the language-shaped reality or intertext of truth in that community.

Like the intertext of anamnesis, this intertext of truth lurks within every sermon to shape the sermon's meanings in often unconscious ways. The semantic code in every sermon rhetorically sponsors (vouches for, promotes, responds to) this intertext in various ways. Every time an idea is expressed in a sermon, it (1) acknowledges the existence of truth in the community, (2) promotes a certain kind of truth in the community, and (3) responds to certain expectations imposed by the form of truth already present in the community. We will look at the ways the semantic code sponsors this intertext of truth shortly.

First, we must ask if preaching contributes anything distinct to the broader intertext of truth in the church. Two observations can be made regarding the uniqueness of the genre of preaching in the sponsoring of truth in the church.

One is that the truth sponsored by preaching is closely related to the way Scripture is interpreted in preaching. As we saw in the previous chapter, sermons cannot be "about" just anything. They must somehow relate their meanings to the biblical testimony. The meaning of a sermon is constrained by the way the original events of the faith witnessed to in Scripture are interpreted and brought over into the contemporary situation.

The second is that the truth sponsored by preaching, to borrow terminology from James Loder, is "four-dimensional."[13] It is not only truth about "lived world" and "self" (two-dimensional truth), but it is patently truth about "the void," or the "potential and inevitable absence of one's being"; and "the holy," or that which is "unique, set apart, and manifest as new being."[14] As we have seen in looking at the categories and predicates for preaching, they are not limited to qualities, relations, natural entities, particular human individuals and groups, nature, and humankind. Preachers are expected to speak also of pure forms, pure states, and transcendent or "ground" beings. Preaching is one of the few remaining public genres of communica-

13. James E. Loder, *The Transforming Moment: Understanding Convictional Experiences* 2d. ed. (Colorado Springs: Helmers & Howard, 1989), 67–91.
    14. Ibid., 67–68.

tion in which listeners expect the orator to speak about the existential and spiritual dimensions of life.[15]

Every preacher makes either conscious or unconscious decisions about how he or she will sponsor the expression of four-dimensional truth in the church. The preacher confronts tremendous difficulties in trying to do this in the face of two-dimensional and reductive worldviews. How do we speak of transcendent or "ground" entities, pure states, or pure forms to people whose worldview considers such things as unverifiable and therefore absurdities? We will look at some of the ways in which preachers attempt to do this in the remainder of this chapter.

STYLES

Let us now look at the ways the semantic code in preaching vouches for, promotes, and responds to the intertext of truth in the church.

Vouching for the Intertext

Several things can undermine the strength of the semantic code in preaching and its ability to vouch for the existence of some form of truth in the community of faith. When the semantic code of a sermon is overburdened with actual or potential subjects and predicates, none of which relates well, or which stand in contradiction one to the other, the semantic code is weakened.

Imagine, for instance, that I decide that I cannot throw out any of the insights I have had while studying the Mary and Martha text in Luke. I attempt to preach a sermon that is simultaneously about the unconventionality of grace, the isolation that results from distraction, the empowerment that Jesus brings to those who are in hiding, the lasting results of new spiritual opportunities seized, the contrast

---

15. John Macquarrie, *Principles of Christian Theology,* 2d ed. (New York: Charles Scribner's Sons, 1977), 146. Macquarrie calls this latter form of truth "existential-ontological" truth. I have chosen the word *spiritual* in order to include also those for whom "ground" beings are conceived as "transcendent." For a discussion of the history of the relationship between *Spirit* and *spirit* and an argument for the latter as more inclusive of all dimensions of the life of spirit, see Paul Tillich, *Systematic Theology,* vol. 3 (Chicago: University of Chicago Press, 1963), 21–30.

between cautious and bold faith, and the fact that all of this could "happen anywhere." Having heard such a sermon, my congregation is likely to go away with the impression that "meaning is whatever strikes your fancy" or with a sense of confusion and meaning anxiety. In such cases, the semantic code is overloaded, overproduced, busy, and cluttered. The content of the semantic code will be more manageable if one meaning is selected, if two or three meanings are combined into one, or if two or three are brought into a clear structural relationship with each other so that they can be handled better by the semantic code of the sermon. Such a change will create a leaner, more focused semantic code that vouches more strongly for the intertext of truth in the sermon.

Another potential problem is hesitancy, lack of clarity, or the choice of insignificant meaning.[16] Overwhelmed by the task of saying something meaningful each week to a congregation, preachers sometimes say to me things like "Who am I to presume to say something to these people?" "No matter what I say, somebody's feathers are going to get ruffled!" or "There are so many things I could say and the biblical text is so alive with meaning that I have a hard time deciding what to say." Any of these concerns can lead to hesitancy, uncertainty, and weak choices when the preacher finally decides what a sermon is to be about. Seminary students, who are usually in a period of conceptual upheaval and preaching in a highly critical situation, often have difficulty deciding what to preach about. Sermons on vague topics like the "presence of God" are typical seminary sermons, where something noncommittal seems to be the safest subject matter.

We live in an era in which theology is in great flux. Traditions are suffering identity crises, and denominations can no longer be easily identified by distinct theological themes. Most preachers find making decisions about the meaning of the gospel difficult in the midst of the great plurality of ideas competing for their attention. What often happens in this situation is that preachers opt for insignificant or

---

16. See Davis, *Design for Preaching*, on significant versus insignificant ideas for preaching.

least-common-denominator ideas.[17] Then the strength of the semantic code suffers. People will sense hesitancy, lack of clarity, and watered-down meaning.

As if to compound these problems, in this era in homiletics conceptual styles of preaching are under considerable fire.[18] In much of homiletical theory today, imagination is opposed to reason, image is opposed to concept, induction is opposed to deduction, and biblical forms of communication are opposed to contemporary forms of communication.[19] Where the use of cognitive and aesthetic subtlety promotes too much ambiguity of meaning before a congregation is ready for it, preaching ceases to vouch for the intertext of truth with any real strength. As we will see, this breakdown does not occur where these styles are carefully negotiated and commensurate with a congregation's style of "holding the true," but where they exist only as fad or experiment the strength of the semantic code can suffer dramatically.

The key to the strength of the semantic code is to have strong and significant ideas that are encoded consistently and clearly. As we will see, these ideas do not have to be encoded deductively or propositionally. Even when they are managed with great sophistication and subtlety, however, they have to reach the level of signification; they have to be signified as meaning in ways that are appropriate to your style and to your congregation's expectations and needs.

Promoting the Intertext

Today the meaning of the gospel is encoded in preaching in a wide variety of ways. Each way of encoding meaning directly or indirectly promotes a similar intertext of truth in the community. For the sake

17. I noted this tendency in recent Presbyterian preaching in my study "Changes in the Authority, Method and Message of Presbyterian Preaching (UPCUSA) in the Twentieth Century," in *The Confessional Mosaic: Presbyterians and Twentieth Century Theology,* ed. Milton J Coalter, John M. Mulder, and Louis B. Weeks (Louisville: Westminster/John Knox Press, 1990).

18. See David Greenhaw, "The Status of Concepts in Preaching" (Paper presented at the Annual Meeting of the Academy of Homiletics, Madison, N.J., 2 December 1988).

19. A good survey article of this trend is Don Wardlaw, "The Need for New Shapes," in *Preaching Biblically: Sermons in the Shape of Scripture* (Philadelphia: Westminster Press, 1983), 11–23.

of clarity and simplicity, I have reduced this plurality to two larger categories of style, what I call *connotative* and *denotative* styles of encoding meaning. Within each of these categories, I will locate two substyles. Within the connotative category are artistic and conversational substyles; within the denotative category are assertive and defensive substyles.

Connotative Style

A dictionary definition of *connote* is "to signify in addition to primary meaning" or "to denote secondarily." Recent studies of connotation, however, show that it is perhaps the primary way of signifying religious meaning.[20] Connotative style is proleptic, that is, expansive, open-ended, and anticipatory. It is communication by juxtaposition, approximation, and substitution. The connotative preacher pays careful attention to ways of combining words into figures of speech such as metaphors and similes in order to probe the boundaries of accepted meaning. Connotative style invites the hearer to discover as much meaning between the lines as in the precise words used. It is a semantic style that invites discussion and dialogue, conversation and participation. It invokes, explores, hints, and insinuates. It points at a meaning rather than "telling"[21] what a meaning is. Connotative style, in the words of Roland Barthes, "corrupts the purity of communication" by "releasing . . . double meaning."[22]

The basic principle of connotative style is semantic motion,[23] which is rooted in the presupposition that religious meaning is not static and fixed but dynamic and fluid. Religious meaning is not univocal. It is not singular, specific, and conforming. Instead, it is "in motion," plurivocal, tensive, and always in a state of transformation. The role of the preacher is to reopen the lexicon of ideas to which the congre-

20. Ricoeur, *Interpretation Theory,* 46–53. Paul Ricoeur debates the assumption that connotation is noncognitive because it is analogical and figurative. He notes how metaphor, at the pinnacle of connotative style, is just as concerned with reference as is denotation.

21. Roland Barthes, *S/Z* (New York: Hill & Wang, 1974), 62.

22. Ibid., 9.

23. Gibson Winter, *Liberating Creation: Foundations of Religious Social Ethics* (New York: Crossroad, 1981), 7; and Philip Wheelwright, *Metaphor and Reality* (Bloomington: Indiana University Press, 1962), 71–72.

gation has grown accustomed, to " 'delexicalize' accepted meanings" and to awaken the congregation to the "instability of meaning, and the possibility of new meaning."[24]

How do we recognize the connotative style in preaching? Connotative style is any style that manages meaning by delaying meaning. We recognize the connotative style because its way of meaning is the way of postponement and prolepsis. We can observe the presence of connotative style in enigmas, promises of answers, requests for answers, snares (deliberate evasions of the meaning, straw answers), equivocations (obvious misdirections), jammings (acknowledgments of the insolubility of the enigma), dialogue with assumed or anticipated meanings, partial answers, or suspended answers (clues).[25] The delay of meaning, however, is not necessarily linear and structural. Delay may be spatial, signified by the use of metaphor, image, story, or conversation at a given moment of the sermon.

The word *delay* does not mean, however, that meaning is not present or does not show up. It simply means that meaning presents itself in a figure, a trope, a conversational trajectory, or a lure toward a final signifier. Indeed, in order for all of these delays to be in any way "meaning-ful," rather than random exercises in intrapsychic musing, they must be oriented toward the disclosure of particular meanings either in or beyond the sermon itself.

A connotative style of encoding meaning promotes a *disclosive* form of truth in the church. Truth is something that is uncovered; it is hidden, concealed. Expectation (prolepsis) is the basic condition of this truth.[26] In other words, truth "is what is at the end of expectation."[27] It arrives. It is the object of desire. It is incarnated in the delay, or what Jacques Lacan calls "error."[28] This form of truth is similar to Heidegger's *alētheia,* "an unveiling which contains its own

---

24. Alan M. Olson, "Myth, Symbol, and Metaphorical Truth," in *Myth, Symbol, and Reality,* ed. Alan M. Olson (Notre Dame, Ind.: University of Notre Dame Press, 1980), 103. See also Paul Ricoeur, *The Rule of Metaphor* (Toronto: University of Toronto Press, 1977), 246.

25. Paraphrased from Barthes, *S/Z,* 210.

26. Ibid., 76.

27. Ibid.

28. Lila J. Kalinich, "The Logos in Lacan," *St. Vladimir's Theological Quarterly* 32 (1988): 373.

veiling, a truth which contains its own untruth."[29] We discover the
true by following its trace in the not yet true. The picture that this
style paints of the community that "holds the truth" is a community
wandering "in error, in forgetfulness of mystery and in falsity of
knowledge."[30] The "lēthe," the forgetfulness at the heart of *alētheia*,
is figured in the delay of connotative style, the concealment or veiling that needs to be lifted if truth is to be manifest.

Artistic Style

The first connotative substyle is the artistic style. In the artistic style,
semantic motion is achieved by semantic innovation.[31] *Innovation*
means "to bring in for the first time." The principle of innovation is
rooted in the presupposition that openness toward religious meaning
cannot be assumed. The meaning of the gospel must therefore be
awakened in the listener. It must be brought in, as if for the first
time. It arrives as an insight, catharsis, or something that makes an
existential claim on the listener.

The preacher with an artistic style of encoding meaning will usually
bring innovative predication to traditional subjects.[32] In preaching
the Mary and Martha text, the artist will be attracted to the unconventionality of Jesus' presence and actions in the home of two women
or to the innovative potential of applying the metaphor of hiding to
the experience of sin by women. However, innovative content is not
enough. The artist then manages this content in a way that brings
that content to light as if for the first time. This content is given over
to innovative and tensive forms of communication. It is expressed as
something that is hidden but now coming to light for us for the first
time.

For instance, the congregation may first of all be encouraged to
reflect on their own involvement with the subject-predicate "sin is
pride." They are invited to reflect on what sin as pride looks like in
everyday experience. Equilibrium is established: a usual subject
appears with its usual predicate. Then, prompted by the scriptural

29. Ibid.
30. Ibid.
31. Winter, *Liberating Creation*, 7.
32. Ricoeur, *Interpretation Theory*, 52. See also D. Lynn Holt, "Metaphors as Imaginative Propositions," *Process Studies* 12 (1982): 252–57.

code, the congregation may be invited to experience the preacher's cognitive dissonance when reading this text under the presupposition that sin is pride. An enigma is presented. Is sin possibly something other than pride? The preacher invites us to consider the fact that although something seems to be wrong with Martha's actions in the text, maybe even sinfully wrong, we cannot seem to find out what it is when we use pride as our definition of sin. Any number of artistic delays will be considered here. For instance, we might introduce a "jam," acknowledging the insolubility of the enigma. We know that sin manifests itself as pride. Just think about the evil consequences associated with those who elevate themselves to the status of gods. If for no other reason, our memories of the Holocaust are too recent to drop the predicate of pride too easily. We could introduce a "snare" or obvious misdirection, considering the possibility that like Martha we can be prideful and self-involved in our efforts to serve others. This argument is weak, of course, because, after all, servanthood is not exactly the best way to live a prideful life. These delays and many potential others confound our powers of reasoning until we innovate, changing our predication of sin in relation to the experience of women. Here the metaphor of hiding is introduced as a clue (partial answer or suspended answer) to the unraveling of meaning. Our artful discovery is complete only when we have reframed the story and our own experience suggestively, not definitively, in terms of hiding, liberation, and empowerment.

Another artistic option is to delay the predication of the meaning of each sequence of the sermon rather than to delay the predication of the meaning of the entire sermon, a *sequential* delay as compared to a *structural* delay. In other words, the larger structure of the sermon could be a series of very clear deductive or topical points. Each point, however, is developed as tensive, nondefinitive, open to question and further development, suggestive, and evocative. When delay is sequential, the artistic stylist of meaning will move, within each sequence of the sermon, into a connotative expansion (jamming, snaring, and the like) and yet resolve this expansion in a suggestive (not definitive) way in each sequence before moving on to the next.

The preacher may decide for a simple topical structure such as:

I. Sin does not mean the same thing for everyone.

II. For women, sin is sometimes experienced as hiding.

III. Grace is disruptive, confrontational, freeing.

In each sequence we know exactly what we are talking about. The subject and predicate of our sequence is clear from the outset. Our artistic task, however, is to break each predicate open, hindering the hearer's tendency toward thematic closure. This task can be accomplished by introducing enigmatic, tensive, or expansive forms of predication for each of our points in order to keep them open-ended and provocative:

I. Is sin the same thing for everyone? (series of delays)

II. How is Martha missing the mark? (series of delays)

III. Sometimes, grace arrives like an unconventional, ill-mannered houseguest.

It could also be accomplished by introducing images, illustrations, and scriptural information early in each sequence in order to delay the arrival of our meaning until the last second.

No matter how sequential delay is introduced, what begins as certain becomes uncertain and open to further semantic exploration. What begins as uncertain and provocative receives further exploration but remains suggestive and open-ended, hinting and insinuating new meanings.

CONSIDERATIONS

The intertext of truth sponsored by the artistic semantic style is an intertext of *epiphanic* truth. Truth is textualized as a "showing forth," a manifestation, happening, or event.[33] It is something that is anticipated and then, within the field of that anticipation, happens to us, shows itself to us, and becomes manifest in our midst.[34] Philosophers

33. See David Tracy, *Plurality and Ambiguity: Hermeneutics, Religion, Hope* (San Francisco: Harper & Row, 1987), 28.

34. See Martin Heidegger, "On the Essence of Truth," in *Basic Writings*, ed. D. Krell (New York: Harper & Row, 1977); Albert Hofstadter, *Truth and Art* (New York: Columbia University Press, 1969); David Farrell Krell, "Art and Truth in Raging Discord: Heidegger and Nietzsche on the Will to Power," in *Martin Heidegger and the Question of Literature: Toward a Postmodern Literary Hermeneutics*, ed. William V. Spanos (Bloomington: Indiana University Press, 1979), 39–53.

have wrestled with how to understand and speak of this kind of truth. For romantic and intuitional philosophers such as Rudolph Otto or Philip Wheelwright, this truth is a totally aconceptual "presential reality."[35] Existential phenomenologist Martin Heidegger speaks in more contemplative and poetic terms of the "presentness of what is present."[36] Philosophical hermeneuticist Paul Ricoeur speaks of it as an "eschatological representation" that is perceived as "a few invaluable, congruent adumbrations which are as the 'pledges of the Spirit.' "[37]

As the language of these philosophers illustrates, the basic problem with this kind of truth lies in its inherent resistance to conceptuality. The artistic delay of meaning that seeks to invoke rather than tell meaning can promote so much ambiguity and subtlety that it can lead to confusion. The problem with a strategy of meaning that is oriented toward the disenfranchisement of assumed meaning is that truth itself can remain in a perpetual state of disenfranchisement. A kind of romance of anticipation can result, a runaway "semantics of desire" in the church and an infatuation with anticipation that ceases to be anticipation *of* anything.[38] At its worst, subjectivism and emotionalism can result. Truth is anything that either builds up or releases pent-up psychic tension and energy. It can also lead to a kind of contrived "artism," an aesthetic dilettantism in the preaching ministry that celebrates "semantic shock"[39] for its own sake.

The obvious strength of this style of encoding meaning is that it promotes a form of truth that is open and conceptually humble. No sacred cows, facile truths, or clichés can survive where this style pre-

35. Wheelwright, *Metaphor and Reality,* 135.

36. Martin Heidegger, *On the Way to Language,* trans. Peter Hertz (New York: Harper & Row, 1971), 15, 34. Quoted in Olson, "Myth, Symbol and Metaphorical Truth," 120.

37. Paul Ricoeur, "Truth and Falsehood," in *History and Truth,* trans. Charles A. Kelbley (Evanston, Ill.: Northwestern University Press, 1965), 182.

38. Deconstructionist thought seems to show an element of this. See, for instance, Charles E. Winquist, *Epiphanies of Darkness: Deconstruction in Theology* (Philadelphia: Fortress Press, 1986), 11–12: "We can then radicalize the subject by ever increasing the range of its significance in experience. There is no self-contained discipline for thinking, because no boundary is immune from limiting questions of what lies beyond its demarcation. The questions are unrestricted, the intention is unrestricted, and the self in its subjective aspect is presented as an unrestricted desire to know."

39. Ricoeur, *Rule of Metaphor,* 296.

dominates. Everything that the community holds as true is open for further investigation and further expansion of meaning. In congregations that have become entrenched in archaic or irrelevant formal systems of thought, this style can come as a breath of fresh air, if it is controlled and negotiated carefully.

NEGOTIATING A HEARING

Preachers come back from workshops on "metaphor and preaching," "imagination and preaching," or "the use of images in preaching" and are met by people who shake their heads and say, "I don't know what the preacher is talking about anymore." People who are used to listening to styles that encode clear and unambiguous conceptual content can feel confused or manipulated by artistic styles of managing meaning in the pulpit. For some people the delay of meaning is perceived as a trick or as a sign of conceptual bankruptcy on the part of the preacher. They expect more definition and redundancy of meaning.

In the face of this kind of expectation, you are wise to include a certain amount of obvious conceptual resolution in your sermons, some clear statement or near-statement of your meaning. Where semantic delay is present, some clear semantic resolution or some clear statement or near-statement of your meaning should also be present. Some narrative and inductive approaches to sermon structure offer a good middle-ground solution to this dilemma.[40] Another possibility would be to mix more denotative sermon structures with artistic sermon sequences, as noted previously. Another intermediate ground, however, is our next connotative semantic style, conversational style.

---

40. See, for instance, narrative models based on either classical narrative approaches or movie or television plots (Eugene Lowry, *The Homiletical Plot: The Sermon as Narrative Art Form* [Atlanta: John Knox Press, 1980]). For an inductive homiletical method, see Fred Craddock, *As One without Authority* (Nashville: Abingdon Press, 1979); and John Broadus, *On the Preparation and Delivery of Sermons*, 3d ed. (New York: Harper & Brothers, 1926), 188–92. Both classical narrative and inductive methods presume some form of semantic resolution. According to Kenneth Seeskin, induction "presupposes agreement on individual cases" (*Dialogue and Discovery: A Study in Socratic Method* [Albany: State University of New York Press, 1987], 30). Narrative presupposes what Barthes calls "a final nomination, the discovery and uttering of the irreversible word" (*S/Z*, 210).

Conversational Style

In the conversational style, the semantic code is governed again by the principle of semantic motion, but it is not achieved as much through semantic innovation as through semantic *reciprocity,* that is, through a movement back and forth among alternative perspectives on a meaning pursued.

Unlike the artistic style, in the conversational style the movement of delay is less art or artifact and less intentional and stylistic. In conversation the movement of delay follows the back-and-forth movement of a dialogue about a potential meaning. Conversation is a rhetoric of listening, of seeking out the "causes of misunderstanding and positing remedies."[41] In conversational delay, questions will be raised, perspectives will be changed, alternatives will be explored, descriptions will be attempted and then abandoned as inadequate or partial, corrections and self-corrections will be made, defenses will be built up and torn down, confrontations will occur and apologies will be offered, and evidence will be stated but not absolutized.

The conversational stylist is not as wary of conceptuality as is the artist. Concepts help to keep the suggestiveness of artistic meaning from degenerating into "mystification."[42] They keep insights accessible to the public arena of discourse, where their appropriateness for the community of faith and their adequacy to the community's experience and theology can be discussed.

This conceptuality, however, is not allowed to atrophy. It is not permitted to solidify into dogma or the demonstration of basic principles. Conceptuality remains conceptuality-in-dialogue, conceptuality that is in search of truth, caught up in the delay, and admitting its partiality and untruth, even as it asserts its conceptual genius.

The preacher does not enter into conversation as a kind of discourse referee who is free from opinions. The preacher's wisdom on a topic is important and must be entered boldly into the conversation. Nevertheless, conversation is neither inductive reasoning nor a

---

41. David J. Hesselgrave, " 'Gold from Egypt': The Contribution of Rhetoric to Cross-Cultural Communication," *Missiology: An International Review* 4 (1976): 95. Hesselgrave paraphrases I. A. Richards, *The Philosophy of Rhetoric,* 3d ed. (London: Oxford University Press, 1971), 3, who urges, "Rhetoric . . . should be a study of misunderstanding and its remedies."
42. Ricoeur, *The Rule of Metaphor,* 313.

mystery novel. The preacher does not have the answers but is simply keeping them to himself or herself. The preacher does not leave a "trail of clues pointing to a single conclusion."[43] In the last analysis, the participation of the preacher as a cosearcher for final truth is vital to the ethos and vitality of the conversational style.

In our sermon on the Mary and Martha text, the sense of missing the mark or *hamartia* in the text can be used as the enigma that energizes our homiletical conversation. The conversationalist, however, will not artfully set up the idea that "sin is pride" for a fall. Sin is assumed at the outset to be understood differently by different people. Resolution to our enigma is pursued through a series of artless conversational delays. Several understandings of sin will be explored in order to include as many people as possible in the conversation. The interpretation of sin as hiding is introduced as one suggestive way of understanding the *hamartia* in the text but not as a resolution to the question of the full nature of sin, for either women or men. Hiding is not an image of resolution but a working hypothesis. We can then go on to examine whether this idea is compatible with our beliefs, what aspects of our experience it addresses, and what consequences it may have for us as a congregation.

CONSIDERATIONS

Conversational style is much needed in situations where reciprocity of meaning is vital to the discovery of common ground for discourse, especially where great plurality of opinion exists or in situations of cross-cultural communication. In theological discourse today, some theologians are calling for a conversational model of interaction between different theological perspectives in order to discover shared meanings.[44] Likewise, missiologists are encouraging a new rhetoric of dialogue and identification on the mission field.[45]

The conversational style in the pulpit sponsors an intertext of

---

43. Seeskin, *Dialogue and Discovery,* 45. Seeskin points out that although Socrates had spent his lifetime in search of the meaning of virtue there is "nothing insincere in Socrates' professing ignorance" on the subject in his dialogues.

44. Tracy, *Plurality and Ambiguity;* and David Tracy and John B. Cobb, Jr., *Talking about God: Doing Theology in the Context of Modern Pluralism* (New York: Seabury Press, 1983).

45. Hesselgrave, "Gold from Egypt," 94–95.

emergent truth. In conversational preaching, truth is not a manifestation or epiphany. It is not a showing forth but a bringing forth. Truth
emerges in the give-and-take of conversation about a topic and
through analysis and synthesis of varying points of view and competing positions. Truth includes both the probable and the plausible.
Truth is a tentative agreement,[46] a momentary consensus, a synthetic
suggestion, or a unifying hypothesis, yet to be tested and proven.

Again, error and concealment occur as truth emerges. With the
consideration of a working hypothesis come new questions, the
awareness of partialities and inadequacies, and the acknowledgment
of unconsidered dimensions, positive and negative, awaiting further
exploration. The conversational style promotes a truth that is very
much "in process."[47] Truth is a significant hunch that provokes a
search that has not yet succeeded and may never be completed.

The uniqueness of this style is that truth emerges as much in the
character of the searchers and the search as in the emergent insights
gained. In conversation, truth is partly virtue. The method of conversation is moral. It builds character that is "true," committed to truth
through honest, engaging, forthright participation in conversation.[48]

Although conversational style does not have the problem of acon-
ceptuality that plagues artistic styles, it does tend toward conceptual
irresolution. Although concepts are arrived at in preaching, they

---

46. Socrates tells Callicles (*Gorgias* 487e) that "any agreement between them would
certainly constitute truth" (Seeskin, *Dialogue and Discovery*, 33).

47. See William A. Christian, *An Interpretation of Whitehead's Metaphysics* (New
Haven: Yale University Press, 1959), 58–59. Process language may be helpful in understanding this kind of truth. For Whitehead, truth is "the conformation of Appearance
(the mental pole of actual occasions, valuations, syntheses, transformations etc.) to
Reality (both contemporary and past occasions)." He makes it clear that, although
truth-relations to past reality can be direct, truth-relations to contemporary reality
"can only be estimated *by an imaginative leap*, which has as its basis for justification
the truth-relations to the past and our experience of the stability of the types of order
involved" (Alfred North Whitehead, *Adventures of Ideas* [New York: Macmillan Co.,
1933], 317–18). The "imaginative leap" required by emergent truth as it relates to
contemporary reality makes its truth claims indirect, partial, and open to further
analysis. In similar fashion, Marjorie Suchocki, in the unpublished paper "The Spoken
Word: The Importance of Proclamation," speaks of how the "proclaimed word which
is heard and the whispered word of our becoming, blend in the operative grace of
God. The hearing of the proclaimed word attunes us to the whispered word we have
always received, and the two words become one in marking out our way."

48. Seeskin, *Dialogue and Discovery*, 136. Seeskin notes that "the connection between virtue and knowledge is at the heart of the Socratic conception of philosophy."

remain hypothetical. They are not permitted to achieve a final status in the community. As such, they may lose both the power to claim a place in the everyday self-expression of the community and thus to motivate a whole community to commitment and action. In other words, truth that is emergent may never finally connect with the lives of an entire community. If hiding is only one hypothetical understanding of sin among many, it may fail to achieve interpretive and expressive power, except for a few people who naturally gravitate toward its meaning. This irresolution can sap its power and deflect its claim on the lives of anyone other than a particular interest group.

On its positive side, however, conversational style yields an intertext of truth that is interactive and therefore inclusive. Truth is open to contributions from everyone, from the greatest to the smallest, from women and men, from all races, nationalities, and persuasions. The "comprehensive, related character of truth"[49] as it emerges in conversation is helpful in the search for unity amidst the diversity and pluralism of today's society.

NEGOTIATING A HEARING

To the person expecting a denotative style of communication, this style will appear as more honest and as less ambiguous than the artistic style. It will still appear, however, to be compromising, sometimes wishy-washy, and perhaps lacking in motivational zeal. When this impression is a problem, you must introduce a certain amount of controlled repetition of new and valued predicates (like hiding) in your preaching. The best way to do this is to reintroduce threads of the same conversation from time to time in relation to varying topics in order to keep an emergent meaning alive as a strong contributing voice in the ongoing conversation of preaching. Through this repetition, a form of predication that remains hypothetical is permitted to gain stronger interpretive and expressive power in the community.

The difficulty in this effort is to prevent the emergent meaning from solidifying and becoming cliché in the community's expressive life. When this happens, conversation is closed off, diversity of opinion is thwarted, and hypothetical predications like hiding become

---

49. Reuel L. Howe, *The Miracle of Dialogue* (New York: Seabury Press, 1964), 121.

sedimented meanings in the community. These meanings will gain denotative power in the form of synergy and ideological fervor but will lose connotative power, the power that comes from combining with other alternatives in favor of still more emergent truth.

The best way to manage this difficulty is to be sure that hypothetical forms of predication are never used as assumptions or as subjects. Keep hypotheses such as hiding in the predicate role. As you work to ensure the repetition of an emergent truth in the community, be sure that it recurs as part of the back and forth of conversation about other topics and never achieves topical status itself.

Denotative Style

The common dictionary definition of *denote* is "to be a name or designation for." The denotation of a word is its primary, accepted dictionary meaning. Denotative style is a style of managing meaning that pushes for correct, accepted, universal meaning. It is a style that seldom combines words into figures of speech in order to avoid ambiguity. It is communication by definition and repetition. It is a style that encourages the making of judgments and argues for particular meanings. It is a style that "tells" what meanings are at every possible juncture to ensure uniformity and clarity. It is preeminently thematic, encouraging hearers to name, define, and own what is being spoken about.

The basic principle of denotative style is "semantic precision."[50] The principle of semantic precision is rooted in the presupposition that religious meanings can be clearly stated and are capable of a certain degree of verifiable accuracy. Religious meanings are univocal and resemble something like "first principles."[51] The role of the preacher is to state clearly and show the veracity of an established lexicon of these first principles, stabilize meanings, and deepen their comprehensive hold on the lives of those in the congregation.

50. Wheelwright, *Metaphor and Reality,* 38.
51. Robert D. Knudsen, "The Transcendental Perspective of Westminster's Apologetic," *Westminster Theological Journal* 48 (1986): 225. Knudsen points out that in Greek the word for "first principle," *archē,* means a major force that "impels and molds" a community.

How do we recognize the denotative style in preaching? Denotative style is any style that manages meaning by *arresting* meaning.[52] We recognize the denotative style because it shows little or no delay in the postulation of meaning. We are not asked to guess or search for what the sermon is about. We are told what it is about in clearly stated themes. The entire sermon contributes in various ways to the demonstration and clarification of these themes. We can distinguish this style by learning to recognize some of the principal means of arresting meaning. Some of the standard rhetorical devices to accomplish these means are postulations, repetitions, arguments of various types, clarifications, definitions, applications, examples, appeals to authority, and descriptions.

The denotative semantic style promotes a *conclusive* rather than disclosive intertext of truth in the church. The intertext of truth is filled with conclusions derived from reflection on certain presuppositions, axioms, or hypotheses.[53] Truth is something that is concluded, an inference reached by the further explication of the already true. It is a finished and final reality that is asserted or defended.

Assertive Style

The first denotative style of preaching is the assertive style. Whereas both artistic and dialogical styles end in insights or hypotheses that may be of potential significance to the congregation, the assertive style turns these insights or hypotheses into assertions[54] and concludes that they are important, justified, worthy of serious ongoing attention, and, in at least a relative sense, necessary to the life of the community.

52. Barthes, *S/Z*, 93. According to Barthes, "a dice throw which can arrest and fix the skid of names: this is thematics."

53. An example of a transcendental premise would be Cornelius Van Til's radical premise that everything that is (being itself) "is possible only on the presupposition of a full-orbed Christian theism" (Knudsen, "The Transcendental Perspective," 228). Foundational premises are apologetic axioms or postulates such as Pannenberg's unifying postulate that "reality itself is essentially historical in character" (Ted Peters, "Truth in History: Gadamer's Hermeneutics and Pannenberg's Apologetic Method," *The Journal of Religion* 55 [1975]: 53).

54. Jürgen Habermas in *Communication and the Evolution of Society* (Boston: Beacon Press, 1979) defines *assertions* as statements that "prima facie imply an unmistakable validity claim, a truth claim" (p. 52). He correlates such statements to the "constatives" in J. L. Austin's speech act theory. See J. L. Austin, *How to Do Things with Words* (Oxford: Oxford University Press, 1962), 144–45.

Assertive style is a committed style. Meanings are no longer suggested, insinuated, or anticipated. They are claimed, affirmed, and confessed. Assertions appear, in the words of Anthony Flew, as "fine brash hypotheses,"[55] unqualified and unapologetic.

Assertive rhetoric is paradigm rhetoric. A paradigm of meaning is a tradition of concepts, examples, and assumptions.[56] Instead of exploring the boundaries of paradigms (artistic style) or the relationships that potentially exist between alternative paradigms (conversational style), assertive style assumes certain complementary paradigms of meaning and then explores the conceptual details of those paradigms. Assertive style demonstrates clear paradigm commitments. In the assertive style, semantic precision is achieved by remaining within the boundaries of particular significant paradigms. Whether a paradigm is a religious tradition such as the Reformed tradition or a contemporary theological, cultural, or scientific paradigm,[57] such as the feminist paradigm or a psychotherapeutic paradigm, once a paradigm has been "taken,"[58] it becomes a focus of

---

55. Anthony Flew and Alasdair Macintyre, eds., *New Essays in Philosophical Theology* (London: SCM Press, 1955), 97–98. Flew critiques these assertions as merely "putative assertions" because they cannot be falsified and therefore cannot be considered as verifiable or true. See Ian Barbour's rebuttal of this argument in *Myths, Models and Paradigms: A Comparative Study of Science and Religion* (New York: Harper & Row, 1976).

56. Thomas Kuhn, *The Structure of Scientific Revolutions*, 2d ed. (Chicago: University of Chicago Press, 1970), 10–52.

57. For paradigm understood as "a tradition transmitted through historical exemplars," see Ian Barbour, *Myths, Models and Paradigms*, 9; and Thomas Kuhn, *The Structure of Scientific Revolutions*, 10–52. For paradigm understood as an "imaginative" (not imaginary) construct, see Garrett Green, *Imagining God: Theology and the Religious Imagination* (New York: Harper & Row, 1989), 66. See also George Lindbeck, *The Nature of Doctrine: Religion and Theology in a Postliberal Age* (Philadelphia: Westminster Press, 1984), 32–45, for a "cultural-linguistic" paradigmatic approach to theology; and Richard A. Rhem, "Theological Method: The Search for a New Paradigm in a Pluralistic Age," *Reformed Review* 39 (1985): 242–53. For potential pitfalls to speaking of religious traditions and constructs as correlative to scientific paradigms, see Cordell Strug, "Kuhn's Paradigm Thesis: A Two-Edged Sword for the Philosophy of Religion," *Religious Studies* 20 (1984): 269–79. I have chosen to use the idea of paradigm instead of the more abstract cultural-linguistic notions of text and "intratext" at this point because the idea of paradigm includes within it the idea of a tradition and community of practice. Paradigms are more than timeless languages or rules of syntax. They are formal systems that find their meanings in communities of commonly shared practice. On the problems associated with Lindbeck's idea of a pure Christian theological grammar, see Lee C. Barrett, "Theology as Grammar: Regulative Principles or Paradigms and Practices," *Modern Theology* 4 (January 1988): 155–72.

58. See Green, *Imagining God*, 68.

energy and commitment. Its language, themes, and conceptual boundaries provide closure to the lexicon of meaning that the preacher pursues.

Underlying the preacher's assertions, then, is a "canon" or paradigm tradition[59] of data and warrants. The preacher has "a lot to go on."[60] He or she is entitled to make certain assertions, given the givens of the paradigm. These givens include the way in which a paradigm tradition uses or interprets Scripture and other key texts; its way of defining key terms, questions, and problems; its way of dealing with anomalies; its key models and exemplars; its typical understanding of human experience; its routine rituals and commitments; and its fundamental theories and concepts.

For instance, to continue our Mary and Martha case, assume that I am committed to both Reformed and feminist theologies and have a commitment as well to transactional analysis. My Reformed background supports the seriousness with which I take sin and the redemptive power of God in Jesus Christ. It also means that I take seriously the Bible, both its "plain sense" and its meaning in its historical context. My feminist commitments provide both data and warrants for the ways in which women and other marginalized people are stripped of power and forced into subordination, assuming hiding as a form of existence. The transactional analysis paradigm provides me a model and theory of an internalized child in each person, forced into hiding by internalized "parents" and desperately in need of "restoration of the freedom to change."[61]

As an assertive stylist of meaning, do I artfully uncover the potentially disclosive power of hiding and empowerment as metaphors for human sin and salvation? Do I suggest that hiding and empowerment are helpful (but not definitive) partners in the ongoing conversation about the nature of human sin and salvation? No! As an assertive stylist, I am prepared to assert clearly and boldly that "Jesus Christ empowers the marginalized to come out of hiding!" I am anxious to repeat this assertion in several ways in this sermon and in other

59. Barbour, *Myths, Models and Paradigms*, 9.
60. Stephen Toulmin, *The Uses of Argument* (Cambridge: Cambridge University Press, 1969), 97.
61. Thomas A. Harris, *I'm OK—You're OK* (New York: Avon, 1969), 83.

sermons. I am ready to reframe this assertion in ways that each of my controlling paradigms suggests. I am eager to support this assertion and bring in supportive data, models, examples, and concepts from within each contributing paradigm. I am ready to deal with anomalies that might come up along the way and to argue for the plausibility, consistency, coherence, importance, and adequacy of this assertion.

CONSIDERATIONS

The assertive style in preaching sponsors an intertext of *decisive* truth. The preacher is like a judge in a courtroom making informed and serious choices. Truth takes the form of a judgment, a decisive ruling, decision, or declaration.[62] The community is not asked simply to entertain or adopt certain truth statements as valid hypotheses or insights. They are asked to decide with the preacher that some truth statements are more promising than others and should be permitted to make truth claims upon the community. These decisive truth claims or judgments take the form of direct assertions, injunctions to believe, or confessions of belief in the life of the congregation itself.[63] They affirm the existence of a community that is "more or less sure" that it has "settled the issue."[64] The congregational mood promoted by this style is one that expects clarity, assurance, and relative stability.[65]

One obvious problem with this style of managing meaning is its resistance to outside influences and criteria for meaning and truth. According to Thomas Kuhn, once a paradigm tradition has been adopted, the community acquires with it the paradigm's own "criterion for choosing problems that . . . can be assumed to have solutions."[66] This outlook can lead to the exclusion of the problems, issues, and concerns that the paradigm does not actively address. For instance, because the issue of a second baptism in the Holy Spirit

---

62. John Wisdom uses this analogy in his famous essay "Gods" (*Philosophy and Psycho-analysis* [London: Basil Blackwell, 1957], 157–58), in which he states that "deciding . . . becomes a matter of weighing the cumulative effect of one group of severally inconclusive items against the cumulative effect of another group of severally inconclusive items."

63. Christian, *Meaning and Truth in Religion,* 143.

64. Ibid., 145.

65. Ibid.

66. Kuhn, *The Structure of Scientific Revolutions,* 37.

does not arise from within the feminist paradigm, it may be left untouched by the preacher who is a committed feminist. Problems of meaning that do not arise from within the paradigm tradition are rejected or avoided. Forms of meaning can result that become insulated and insensitive to the concerns of those who represent other paradigms of meaning. Such meanings can be perceived as truncated, naive, and uncritical.[67]

Another problem with this style is that it often promotes a willful lack of originality that can lead to prejudice. Paradigm practitioners are mostly involved in what Kuhn calls "mop-up work." Seldom do they aim at new theories, and they are "often intolerant of those invented by others."[68] A certain amount of intolerance is to be expected and must be accepted with commitment to a paradigm. Preachers, however, can become so excited about the minutiae of potential shared meanings within one paradigm tradition that they cease to explore the boundaries of the paradigm. They are satisfied to repeat tried-and-true axioms. They can easily lose sight of the limitations of the paradigms on which they rely. Then, other paradigms can begin to look more and more suspicious, even sinister. Moderate intolerance changes into wholesale prejudice.

The obvious strength of this style of encoding meaning in sermons is that it promotes clarity and precision. Even when the preacher's paradigms do not match those of members of the congregation, this style brings out the paradigm dependency of everyone in the congregation. When a preacher asserts as a definitive truth claim that "Jesus empowers the marginalized to come out of hiding," people suddenly have to ask themselves, "Do I really think that?" The fact that the preacher is assertive brings out the assertiveness of the congregation, either in unity with or in debate against the preacher. Clarification and precision become issues for the community. Where a paradigm fit between the preacher and congregation is present, assertive style

67. Barbour, *Myths, Models and Paradigms,* 110–33, 142–46. From the scientific community Barbour extrapolates such criteria as (1) the presence of common data, (2) the cumulative effect of evidence for or against a theory, and (3) the existence of criteria that are not paradigm-dependent that show up in religion as (1) the assessment of alternative religious or naturalistic paradigms, (2) self-criticism of one's own basic beliefs, and (3) communication between paradigm-communities.

68. Kuhn, *The Structure of Scientific Revolutions,* 24.

simply reinforces and further hones the meanings that are a part of that paradigm and keeps them clear and precise. In either case, this style communicates that what the community holds as true needs to be unambiguous and unequivocal.

Another benefit is the amount of depth and detail of meaning that assertive style can bring to preaching. A "promise of success"[69] is inherent in paradigm-dependent communication, based upon a previous tradition of success and the building up of a detailed shared vocabulary.[70] Therefore, very minute dimensions of religious experience and reality can be explored at great depth.

Assume that I am committed to a feminist theological paradigm and assert the premise that hiding is a very real *hamartia* in the experience of women and that Jesus Christ wants to break through the walls behind which this hiding occurs. Banking on a tradition of research, concepts, theories, and examples provided by the feminist theological paradigm, I can investigate with great depth and detail the validity and transforming power of this assertion. I can relate this assertion to a huge body of data on the internal dynamics of spouse abuse, sexual exploitation, ordination of women, human rights, and many other issues.

Another benefit of assertive style is that, once a relative semantic match or fit has been achieved between the congregation and the preacher, this style promotes social cohesion, self-awareness, and a heightened sense of communal identity. The congregation becomes a group of people who "know what it is about." Such a community is more likely to commit itself to certain forms of action and behavior, if only to provide further data and warrants for its truth claims. The assertive style, then, can be a style that motivates and secures actions in conformity with a paradigm. As unity increases, the ability to motivate increases.

---

69. Ibid., 23.
70. A good historical example of this is the role of Thomas Cranmer's *Homilies* (1547) in the Anglican church and Charles Wesley's *Sermons* (1771–1772) in the Methodist church. See Richard P. Heitzenrater, "Plain Truth: Sermons as Standards of Doctrine," *Drew Gateway* (Fall 1987): 16–30.

NEGOTIATING A HEARING

Two overlapping types of problems can occur in negotiating a hearing for the assertive style. One is a content problem; the paradigm being asserted is in direct conflict with another (or several other) assertive paradigms in the community. A second problem is a style problem; the congregation is used to a more artistic or dialogical style that delays meaning and is suddenly confronted with a bold attempt to arrest meaning.

In order to overcome problems that arise from conflicts of meaning between paradigms, the preacher will need to look initially for compatible meanings between paradigms. These areas are where discord will be least and where the preacher can focus efforts to crossbreed paradigms. Returning to areas of agreement or near-agreement will lessen tension and allow for some movement back and forth between paradigms.

For instance, the feminist understanding of Jesus as empowerer does not have to be construed as antithetical to the evangelical understanding of Jesus as forgiver of sins. The preacher can focus on the active, empowering, freeing side of forgiveness. To support empowerment does not necessitate denying the validity and importance of forgiveness. In the Mary and Martha text, for example, the presence of Jesus (the forgiver) provokes immediate empowered action on Mary's part. It also provokes a reaction of worry and anxiety from Martha. The empowered response (to the forgiver) is what becomes "the good portion that cannot be taken away." The preaching of other texts, in which forgiveness is more self-evident, will provide stronger opportunities to draw out this compatibility. For instance, in Mark 2:1-12, when Jesus forgives the paralytic his sins, he closely relates his offer of forgiveness to the empowering words "rise, take up your pallet and go home." A compatibility between forgiveness and empowerment can be established in sermons on many biblical texts and thus provide a point of relationship between two potentially conflicting paradigms of meaning.

When new and obviously conflicting aspects of a new paradigm are first being introduced, the preacher may want to mix assertive style with conversational and artistic styles. The preacher can learn from these styles how to be suggestive by presenting a new meaning initially as an insight or hypothesis, exploring its boundaries, and establishing supporting data and warrants that do not already exist in the community. The preacher will learn how to open up semantic space for a new meaning by artistically juxtaposing a new predicate with an already existing subject. A new meaning may take some time to gain enough acceptance to become a strong assertion in the preacher's sermons.

No matter how carefully the preacher negotiates, however, some paradigm conflict will always occur when the assertive style is the basic style of managing homiletical meaning. One frame of reference is always in a certain amount of tension with another. This result is not necessarily negative. As we have already seen, in this way the assertive style makes semantic clarification and precision active issues in a community.

Concerning style conflict, some people, perhaps with good reason, will hear assertiveness as pushiness. They are probably people who come to preaching with more connotative expectations for meaning. They are listening for the inclusion of a wide range of ideas and opinions. They do not mind hearing their own paradigm supported, but they want to hear from paradigms other than their own; or they do not mind entertaining the ideas of another paradigm, but they want to hear their own appreciated and brought into the discussion. Perhaps they are simply looking for new insight. They are tired of the same old thing and have begun to expect new insights to be brought in by the preacher. Where these conversational and artistic expectations are strong, the assertive style will fall on troubled and unresponsive ears.

The preacher who senses these expectations will at least want to explore the boundaries of his or her dominant paradigm(s) from time to time, note places of possible overlap and conversation with other paradigms, and entertain new insights. As we have noted, this process is healthy and even necessary, a way of keeping paradigms self-critical and tuned in to contemporary problems and concerns. The number of anomalies in the current paradigm may have become so troublesome and irresolvable that the preacher will seriously entertain what Kuhn calls a "paradigm shift" or a conversion to another or a modified paradigm.[71]

71. Kuhn, *The Structure of Scientific Revolutions*, 52–136.

Defensive Style

I have chosen the word *defensive* instead of the word *apologetic* for this style because the word *apologetic* has been applied more to theology than to preaching and rhetoric in the last century and has broadened somewhat in its meaning.[72] Modern theological apologetics is mainly concerned to "relate theology to culture."[73] Traditional rhetorical apologetics, however, was more concerned to vindicate the very reality and truth of the Christian faith. In its early usage in the Christian church, the word *apologia* simply meant "defense." When attacks were made against the teaching and preaching of an apostle or when he was called upon to reply to a specific charge made against him, he "made his defense" (ἀπελογεῖτο, Acts 26:1).[74]

The defensive homiletical stylist goes beyond asserting the worthiness, adequacy, and importance of certain meanings to declare their absolute universality and objectivity. The preacher becomes a strict "semantic positivist,"[75] insisting on singular meanings for singular words and concepts. Such a posture is usually possible only when the preacher is certain that he or she is proclaiming meaning that is not only "paradigmatic" but also "transcendental" in nature.[76] In the words of Robert D. Knudsen of Westminster Theological Seminary, the presuppositions for apologetic discourse are "not simply intellectually formulated principles, on the order, let us say, of theoretical axioms. Nor are they simply postulates, which may be drawn from theology as a scientific discipline."[77] They are "radicals" or "transcendentals," without which there could be no meaning (or being) at all.[78]

72. Norman Sykes, "Some Current Conceptions of Historiography and Their Significance for Christian Apologetic," *The Journal of Theological Studies* 50 (1949): 24–198; and Ralph E. Knupp, "The Apologetic Preaching of Paul Tillich," *Encounter* 42 (1981): 395–407.
73. Knudsen, "The Transcendental Perspective," 226.
74. Paraphrased from Frederic R. Howe, "Kerygma and Apologia," in *Jerusalem and Athens: Critical Discussions on the Theology and Apologetics of Cornelius Van Til*, ed. E. R. Geehan (Philadelphia: Presbyterian and Reformed Publishing Co., 1971), 446; Paul Tillich, "The Apologetic Movement," in *A History of Christian Thought* (New York: Harper & Row, 1968), 24–32; and Richard Tatlock, *Proving Preaching and Teaching* (London: Faith Press, 1963).
75. Wheelwright, *Metaphor and Reality*, 38.
76. Knudsen, "The Transcendental Perspective," 227.
77. Ibid.
78. Ibid., 227–28.

The principal way in which meaning is arrested in the defensive style is through argument. Semantic precision is achieved through the argument for singular and final meanings. Even though transcendentals would seem to be beyond argument, they must nonetheless be defended, which means that they must be argued and shown to be absolutely final and necessary. Instead of incorporating occasional arguments or relying periodically on past arguments, the defensive style grants argument a controlling status in the way that meaning is presented in the sermon. Instead of relying on a tradition of warrants and data to make positive assertions, the preacher introduces all kinds of backing from Scripture, tradition, experience, and science to support his or her radical truth claims.

The defensive stylist, in the Mary and Martha sermon, would harden the predicate of "empowerer of the marginalized" into an absolute and final predicate for the subject of "Jesus Christ." For this stylist, many forces in our culture, our society, the theological academy, and our own church would dilute, deny, or destroy this absolute truth. Therefore, it must be defended with as much rhetorical energy as is necessary.

Several things will stand out in this kind of rhetoric. First of all, faulty, competing ideas will be stated, dismantled, and discarded as inaccurate and inadequate. Defensive style is oppositional style. It must at some point acknowledge its opponents and deflect their attacks.

Second, this style will go beyond paradigm arguments for the relative adequacy, consistency, and coherence of certain meanings. It will argue for the logical *necessity* of its meanings. This style goes beyond saying that a particular predicate is true for a particular subject. It means arguing that a predicate is factually true for that subject and that subject alone. For example, the defensive stylist will be to some degree committed to the argument that, when all else has been said, "empowerer" is ultimately the correct predicate for Jesus Christ and for Jesus Christ alone. When "empowerer" is applied to any other subject, it is metaphorical and connotative; when we apply it to Jesus Christ, it is an actual name for him. It defines him in a clear, one-to-one correspondence. For the defensive stylist, the word *empowerer* has become an absolutely necessary predicate for Jesus Christ.

Third, testing is an important rhetorical figure in defensive rhetoric. In order to prove the necessity of its meanings, this style must display (at least rhetorically) some willingness to have its truth claims tested. In many cases, sermons will include some actual tests. The criteria for these tests will vary. Some tests will show an inductive correspondence between a meaning and relevant observations. For instance, the preacher will observe that Christianity is growing where poor and marginalized people are discovering in Christ an empowerer in the struggle for freedom. This observation confirms the validity of the preacher's truth claim. Another test is the test for logical noncontradiction. In this test, Christ the empowerer will be proven to be in noncontradiction to the full range of the biblical witness and human experience. Yet another test is the test for existential viability. In this test, Christ the empowerer will be shown to be adequate to answer the major existential and spiritual questions that arise from human experience.[79]

CONSIDERATIONS

The defensive style in preaching sponsors an intertext of *final* or *factual* truth. The preacher is like a competent experimental researcher repeating certain experiments in order to shore up the finality of certain carefully proven facts. The community is not asked to decide on the relative accuracy or inaccuracy of certain assertions within a particular paradigm of meaning. Instead, they are asked to adopt certain assertions as final and definitive facts and to participate in the recurring defense of these facts against a variety of competing assertions.

One obvious problem with this style is its propensity to grant ultimate and final status to meanings that are, in actuality, dependent upon shifting paradigms and historical milieus. Whether the Westminster Confession, the documents of the World Council of Churches, or a preacher's own synthetic theological pronouncements become the irreversible word that the church must accept as final, at least the possibility of some degree of error and inconsistency always exists in any such word. The idolization of human rationality is always

---

79. For a good survey of "methods of justifying belief," see Gordon R. Lewis, "Schaeffer's Apologetic Method," in *Reflections on Francis Schaeffer*, ed. Ronald W. Ruegsegger (Grand Rapids: Zondervan, 1986), 70–87.

a potential problem where defense of final truth is the platform upon which preaching stands.

Although the defensive style is, at least in principle, open to rational criteria for assessment and verification of its assumptions, another problem is that it seldom is. Transcendental presuppositions usually preclude other kinds of proofs than those that are consistent with their premises. In essence, neither confirmation nor disconfirmation of these presuppositions is possible. Proofs are offered according to the rules of the game only, and defense easily degenerates into diatribe.

The defensive stylist must also be aware of the great potential for boredom that comes with the repetition of arguments. An experiment that proves a fact can be varied in only a few small ways. Likewise, arguments can be made only in one or two really convincing ways. Congregations tend to hear preachers repeat the same arguments over and over again. People are literally worn down by this repetition. Even when these arguments are charged with great negative emotion and people grunt with satisfaction over the perils of humanism or the sins of the patriarchy, the redundancy of such arguments can become boring and even banal.

Perhaps the most significant problem with defensive rhetoric is its negativity. Although most apologetic communicators will attest to positive intentions, their defensive posture and argumentative tone usually convey the opposite. Selected opponents loom large in this kind of discourse, whether they be the "liberals," the "humanists," the "fundamentalists," the "patriarchy," the "oppressors," or whomever. A clear "us" and a clear "them" can lead, again, to exclusivity, prejudice, and even hatred of opponents.

On the positive side, the defensive style, like the assertive style, supports thematic clarity and precision in preaching. It also heightens a congregation's sense of identity and its commitment to particular forms of action and behavior.

Beyond this, however, is the very real fact that aspects of the Christian faith do need defense from time to time from counterclaims that seek to deny them any modicum of factuality or finality in human life. Christians need to be able to defend their faith when it is seriously challenged. They need to know that they both can and should defend their beliefs when called upon to do so. In many

churches today, defense is much needed and sought after by belea-
guered Christians who are confronted daily by friends, family, and
colleagues who have very different values and assumptions about
life. The defensive style of preaching can support a congregation's
needs for arguments in behalf of their beliefs and their need for a
strong community of support in the making of such arguments. For
this to be a positive phenomenon, however, what is communicated
must not be narrow backbiting or vindictive stereotyping but a way
of arguing that, although energized by a sense of the finality of Christian truth, remains open to an ongoing assessment and upgrading of
the arguments in light of new information.

NEGOTIATING A HEARING

Obviously, the defensive stylist will need to be aware of all of the
problems encountered by the assertive stylist. Unlike the assertive
stylist, however, the defensive stylist is typically not amenable to
step-by-step negotiations of either substance or style. When we
assume transcendental presuppositions, taking competing truth claims
seriously becomes difficult.

Again, where congregational expectations are mixed, I urge a mixing of styles and the crossbreeding of substance prior to deciding or
settling for a particular paradigm of meaning. If this paradigm is
determined to require the strength of rhetorical "finality"[80] in the
community or if some defenses and arguments are needed to pre-
serve its integrity and forcefulness, then the defensive style may be
introduced as a supplementary style.

APPLYING THE SEMANTIC CODE

We have now had an opportunity to examine the semantic code and
the four principal ways in which this code sponsors the intertext of
truth in the church today. The second layer of our rhetorical schema
looks like this:

---

80. For other than "transcendental" ways of envisioning this "finality," see Don
Cupitt, "On the Finality of Christ," in *The Leap of Reason* (Philadelphia: Westminster
Press, 1976), 119–31.

Semantic Code

Content: Anything in a sermon that signifies meaning: principally categories of thought and sermon ideas (subjects and predicates)

Intertext: Truth, what the congregation "holds as true" and the way that this truth is held

Styles: Code styles sponsor intertext styles (Table 5)

TABLE 5
Semantic Code and Intertext Styles

Code Style	Sponsors	Intertext Style
Connotative		*Disclosive truth*
1. Artistic		1. Epiphanic truth (manifestation)
2. Conversational		2. Emergent truth (hypothesis)
Denotative		*Conclusive truth*
1. Assertive		1. Decisive truth (judgment)
2. Defensive		2. Final truth (fact)

In this chapter I have suggested that preaching sponsors in four basic styles a lexicon of meaning in the church that is shaped by Scripture and four-dimensional in nature. Let me now suggest again a broader analytical process for the preacher to try in order to achieve strategic strength in the encoding of meaning in sermons.

Homiletical Analysis

Begin the process with an analysis of the content and style of the semantic code in your preaching. Use this adaptation of J. R. Nichols's idea inventory[81] to analyze your semantic content over the past year, listing your basic seven (plus or minus two) sermon ideas.

---

81. J. R. Nichols, *Building the Word* (New York: Harper & Row, 1980), 53–58, 135–40.

1. Select a group of sermons. This past year's sermons would be a good starting point; if you have time, two years would be better.

2. Scan. Get a pad of paper and try not to think very much about what you are about to do. Read quickly through your sermons, notes, or outlines. A quick scan will usually bring them back to mind. Jot down a single phrase or word that describes the focal concern of the sermon. The list will end up with as many entries as there are sermons in your sample. For instance,

Loss of joy
Crisis brings opportunity
Mystery
Demands of the world
God's healing is different
Worry—good and bad
What kids think about God

3. Observe and report. Sit back and read through the list several times. Begin to notice groupings of the words, phrases, or sentences that seem to bear a general family resemblance to each other. You might notice, for instance, that of the sermons you analyze, groups or clusters of topics begin to emerge, something like

Commitment and dedication
Personal involvement
Ministry is for everyone
Being "for" other people
Crisis is opportunity
Disciples—Jesus' calling them
The meaning of Christian care

Don't be too specific yet. Note general clusters. Don't "think" too much yet. Just observe and report.

4. Analyze. Now begin to think—not like a theologian, but like a detective. Sort your list of tentative family groupings carefully. Group them together according to themes or ideas or master images or underlying thoughts that seem to make them lump together. You may wind up with a dozen or more; you may wind up with three or four.

5. *Inventory*. Go through and name each of the governing ideas. Do this in two ways.

1. A noun that was basic to the category
2. A sentence of direct address to translate that underlying abstraction into message form

For example;

Subject	*Basic Message*
Emotions	Empathy and love are the keys to Christian life
Christ	Christ is God's love victorious over the power of sin, evil, and death
Church	The church is a new reality—a community ruled by love not law
Acceptance	God accepts you and loves you just as you are
Action	We can make a difference in the world
Outcomes	God helps us to be more than we ever thought we could be

6. *Checkup*. Go back to a group of sermons not included in your first sampling and see whether the categories apply. This sampling could be more recent. You may discover that your preaching has grown in the last few months and the categories have shifted slightly, or you may discover that in the last six months you have preached only two categories.

Do not be put off by renegade sermons that do not seem to fit anywhere. Look carefully at them and see if they do not divide into several of your categories all at once.

Next, analyze your sermon style by using the four categories of artistic, conversational, assertive, and defensive (see the concluding chapter for an example of this kind of sermon decoding). Again, if you do not use a manuscript, you may want to tape your sermons for a few months and transcribe them so that they can be studied more easily.

Congregational Analysis

The second step is to gain some understanding of the basic lexicon of meanings and stylistic expectations of your congregation. In order to accomplish this, I encourage you to put together a series of sermon-planning groups that would last for a six- to eight-month period. Each group should have eight to ten members and should meet with you only for six weeks. Then change the group so that by the end of an eight-month period you have sampled a fairly large and diverse portion of your congregation.

This group's purpose is to help you prepare your sermons for each Sunday. Have them look at the biblical text, jot down their insights, thoughts, and ideas, and share them with you. This group is an idea group, not an exegesis group. They will discuss with you the biblical text and ideas that you might consider for your preaching. Your job is to tape-record each session. Later, go back through all of these tapes and do the same kind of content analysis or idea inventory that you have done for your sermons to determine at the end of the eight-month period your congregation's basic seven (plus or minus two) ideas for preaching.

As a part of each of these group meetings, ask the members of the group style-oriented questions also, questions such as

1. How would you preach these ideas?
2. Do you think I would have to be careful in how I say things?
3. How forceful do you think I should be with ideas like this?
4. Do you think these ideas are important enough for me to defend in the pulpit?

You may also simply ask them which style of preaching of the four categories discussed they prefer. From these questions you should be able to determine what general style your congregation looks for and the amount of diversity of expectation it has.

Theological and Pastoral Analysis

The third step is to analyze theologically and pastorally what you are doing and what you need to do.

Theological Reflection

Here you will want to examine your understanding of the nature and function of religious language. You can read several books[82] on this subject to supplement the others you can find throughout the notes for this chapter.

After your reading, ask yourself several questions. First of all, do you see religious language as principally metaphorical and symbolic in an evocative sense? Is religious language fundamentally a language of participation rather than the language of interpretation or definition? Do you see religious language as dramatic language that has the primary function of opening up a kind of "liminal" or "between-worlds" space in which the holy can be experienced and perceived as present?[83] If, after studying religious language, you decide that religious language is basically metaphorical and symbolic in this sense, you will want to give serious attention to the artistic style that most closely represents these commitments.

Do you instead see religious language as symbolic and metaphorical in an interpretive sense? Do you believe that religious language actually refers to specific realities, yet in indirect and tensive ways? Do you believe that these symbolic and metaphorical references create communities of discourse that seek to understand further and articulate conceptually the reality referred to? If this is your understanding of religious language, you will want to give serious attention to artistic, conversational, and assertive styles, depending on the degree of conceptuality and exclusivity you are willing to grant to your particular interpretive language.

Finally, do you believe that religious language is directly referential? In your understanding of religious language, does it name and

82. Besides books of interest in the preceding notes, see Ian Ramsay, *Religious Language: An Empirical Placing of Theological Phrases* (London: SCM Press, 1957); Langdon Gilkey, *Naming the Whirlwind: The Renewal of God-Language* (Indianapolis: Bobbs-Merrill, 1969); Phyllis Trible, *God and the Rhetoric of Sexuality* (Philadelphia: Fortress Press, 1978); Sallie McFague, *Metaphorical Theology: Models of God in Religious Language* (Philadelphia: Fortress Press, 1982); Gordon H. Clark, "Inspiration and Language," in *Religion, Reason and Revelation* (Philadelphia: Presbyterian and Reformed Publishing Co., 1961); and Paul Tillich, *Dynamics of Faith* (New York: Harper & Brothers, 1957).

83. For further definition of the liminal and antistructural nature of religious language, see Victor Turner, *The Ritual Process: Structure and Antistructure* (Chicago: Aldine Publishing, 1969) and *Dramas, Fields and Metaphors: Symbolic Action in Human Society* (Ithaca, N.Y.: Cornell University Press, 1974).

define with near or complete precision the reality to which it refers? In this case, you will want to devote your energies to assertive and defensive styles, depending on the type and level of referential accuracy you wish to claim for religious language.

Pastoral Reflection

As a pastor, you will first need to reflect on your basic homiletical ideas in relation to the ideas that are significant to your congregation. Are they similar? Where are the big differences? What are the conflicts? What are they listening for that is missing in your lexicon of ideas? What are you preaching that they are clearly not listening for or seem even to care about? How do you evaluate your lexicon? Is it clear, consistent, and theologically sound? What about the congregation's lexicon? Is it clear, consistent, and theologically sound?

From this series of questions you should identify semantic areas that need development or change. You should begin to note places where you are theologically weak or inconsistent. You should spot some instances where you and your congregation are butting heads. You should begin to see new avenues of meaning that both you and your congregation can explore together.

The second thing you should do is to reflect on your semantic style and the expectations that exist in your congregation. Is your congregation hungry for more openness and more creative exploration of new meanings? Are they in need of dialogue with other paradigms of meaning? Are they desperate for more assertiveness, clarity, and commitment from the pulpit? Do they feel as if they are under constant attack and need clear arguments for their beliefs?

Conscious Commitment

The final step in your process is to commit yourself consciously to a particular style of encoding meaning in preaching. Focus your continuing education and homiletical reading around that style. Commit yourself also to a lexicon of ideas that will meet the needs of your congregation at this time.

If this larger process is too much for you to try at this time, reflect on your current semantic style. Consider ways to strengthen this style and to negotiate a better hearing for it. Ask yourself if it is true to your theological commitments and the needs of your congregation. Think of ways in which you can broaden or focus your lexicon of ideas so that it will respond more dynamically to the kinds of ideas that are important to members of your congregation. Above all else, as you prepare sermons, try to become conscious and strategic in the way that you manage meaning in your preaching.

3

THE THEOSYMBOLIC CODE

Embedded within the preacher's semantic lexicon is the theosymbolic code, which is reflected in the preacher's semantic efforts but is not equal to them.[1] Whereas the semantic code is in many ways a product of the preacher's reactions or commitments to various theological and nontheological paradigms of meaning, the theosymbolic code represents the emergent or full-blown theological model or structure that manifests itself in the language of the preacher's sermons.[2] It is the preacher's own synthetic theological product.

1. See Paul Ricoeur, *Interpretation Theory: Discourse and the Surplus of Meaning* (Fort Worth: Texas Christian University Press, 1976), 61–88, on the relationship between metaphor and symbol. Metaphor, or semantic innovation, is "a free invention of discourse"; symbols are "bound to the cosmos." In other words, symbols have both a "semantic face" and a "non-semantic one." In this sense, the semantic code is only one face of the theosymbolic code. It "brings to language the implicit semantics of the symbol."

2. A model is a complex or set of symbols that embodies the fundamental relationships between various entities or processes. See Clifford Geertz, *The Interpretation of Cultures: Selected Essays* (New York: Basic Books, 1973), 91–92. According to Ian Barbour, *Myths, Models and Paradigms: A Comparative Study of Science and Religion* (New York: Harper & Row, 1976), 6, a model is "a symbolic representation of selected aspects of the behavior of a complex system for particular purposes." Sallie McFague (*Metaphorical Theology: Models of God in Religious Language* [Philadelphia: Fortress Press, 1982]) points out that language models are closer to "theoretical models" than to "scale models." Theoretical models amount to what Max Black (*Models and Metaphors* [Ithaca, N.Y.: Cornell University Press, 1962], 243) calls "talking in a certain way" about certain things. My use of the word *structure* in relation to model highlights my primary interest in the system of relations that compose a model rather than in the semantic content. I am interested in models more as systems than as metaphors.

Because of the more limited range of the preacher's ideas and commitment to particular ideas for pastoral reasons, the preacher's theological model will seldom represent the full scope of a major systematic theological paradigm. In other words, major theological paradigms are usually abbreviated and adapted in preaching. At the same time, as we have already seen, preachers usually draw upon several theological and nontheological paradigms of meaning in their preaching, which further dilutes the purity of the preacher's own theological model in the pulpit.

CONTENT

In the words of cultural anthropologist Clifford Geertz, symbols are "ideas, attitudes, judgements, longings or beliefs" that have been "concretely embodied" or "fixed in perceptible forms."[3] Preachers are not entirely free like poets or hierophants to explore the full range of primitive symbolic archetypes. Christian sacred symbols and the theological models in which these symbols function are pregiven by the larger theological paradigm of Scripture and the traditions of the church. The Christian, for instance, already has many symbols of the power and character of God: the creation, the burning bush, the covenant, the Torah, and the incarnation. Christians already have symbols for the activity of sin and evil in human life: the Fall, the tower of Babel, Job, the Gerasene demoniac, and the temptation of Jesus by Satan in the wilderness. Christians already have symbols of redemption: the dove and the rainbow, the parting of the Red Sea, the promised land, and the empty tomb.

These and other pregiven symbols are for the Christian nonnegotiable, except in their interpretation. As we have seen in the previous chapter on semantics, various meanings can be provoked, hypothesized, asserted, or defended for each of these root symbols. The biblical text can be explored for new interpretations of each category of symbol. We saw, for example, how the Mary and Martha text suggests that sin could be interpreted in a new way as hiding.

3. Geertz, *The Interpretation of Cultures*, 91.

At the theosymbolic level, we are no longer concerned with the process whereby biblical symbols are interpreted (scriptural code) and become meaningful and in some sense "true" in the community (semantic code). At this level we are concerned with the *ordering* of these symbols into a particular model or structure of meaning. In other words, we are now interested in the roles theological symbols play in a larger theological structure that exists in the preacher's homiletical rhetoric.

Beyond establishing that "sin is hiding" is important and in some sense true for the community, this idea is placed in an ordered relationship with other ideas as part of the preacher's larger theological structure. In other words, this idea will be given a role typical of the role that sin usually plays in the preacher's larger theological structure, no matter how it is conceptualized. For example, if the preacher typically pictures sin in a very large and powerful role in the theological structure, the sin of hiding will likewise play a very large and powerful role. If the preacher pictures sin as something that exists only to be exploited in order to show the power and grace of God, the sin of hiding will likewise be seen as an opportunity to show forth the wonders of redemption.

How can we understand this larger theological structure so that we can grasp more clearly the various roles that theological symbols tend to play in homiletical rhetoric? Because preaching is rooted in Scripture, this larger theological structure can be understood broadly as a narrative structure.[4] Scripture, in the words of Garrett Green, is the "normative vision" for all of the theological paradigms of the Christian community.[5] All Christian theological paradigms must be

---

4. According to Jean Piaget (*Structuralism,* trans. and ed. Chaninah Maschler [New York: Basic Books, 1970]), the word *structure* means a "system of transformations." The structural level at which symbolic systems are determined is the macrolevel of the mythical system rather than the microlevel of the narrative system. For this reason, I have superimposed the mythic structure (Lévi-Strauss) onto the narrative structure of A. J. Gremais (in a very simplified fashion) in order to draw forth the symbolic oppositions and mediations from the narrative structure. For a more detailed and scientific approach to this, see Daniel Patte, *What Is Structural Exegesis?* (Philadelphia: Fortress Press, 1976), 21–34; and Daniel Patte and Aline Patte, *Structural Exegesis: From Theory to Practice* (Philadelphia: Fortress Press, 1978), 11–38.

5. Garrett Green, *Imagining God: Theology and the Religious Imagination* (New York: Harper & Row, 1989), 105.

in some way responsive and responsible to Scripture and, in particular, to the gospel of Jesus Christ.

The gospel is basically a narrative structure framed within a larger narrative structure that includes not only the great stories of the mighty acts of God but also "creation, and with it the universal ('general') revelation of the kind implicit in the patterns of truth manifest in the wisdom literature, in the piety of Psalms, and in the problem of Job."[6] This larger narrative ultimately moves beyond the text of Scripture and embraces the history and experience of the church. It becomes the church's own faith story, which the church narrates from the point of view of the turning point in the narrative—as those who are "in Christ."[7]

Seen in this manner, the preacher is a community narrator, telling the church's faith story as one who is in Christ. No matter what the preacher's theological paradigm, it conforms to the basic narrative structure of this Christian faith story.

The faith story or narrative structure embedded in a preacher's sermons is populated by key characters who play certain roles. These characters correspond to the major categories of Christian theological symbols. These characters do not necessarily have to be people or personal entities. Narrative structuralist A. J. Gremais calls them *actants*. Actants are "structural constants," or basic spheres of narrative action.[8] Their roles in the larger narrative are what is most important. An easy way to see these characters or actants and the theological content they represent within the narrative structure of the Christian faith story is to make use of the insights of Gremais. According to Gremais, there are six essential narrative characters or actants.

1. The giver or sender. The arbiter or rewarder in a narrative. The Giver in the Christian faith story corresponds principally to God and to all the symbolic events or actions of God in the broader Christian

---

6. Gabriel Fackre, *The Christian Story: A Pastoral Systematics,* vol. 2 (Grand Rapids: Wm. B. Eerdmans, 1987), 180.

7. Ibid. See also D. Buttrick, *Homiletic: Moves and Structures* (Philadelphia: Fortress, 1989), 15. As Buttrick puts it, "In Christ, the genre of the Christian faith-story is *gospel.*"

8. Patte, *What Is Structural Exegesis?* 42.

narrative (doctrine of God, doctrine of creation, doctrine of the Trinity, predestination, providence).

2. The receiver. The ultimate beneficiary of the narrative, who usually sends the hero on the quest. The receiver corresponds to humanity and to creation as they are symbolically depicted in the broader Christian narrative (theological anthropology, doctrine of creation).

3. The object. The desired object in the narrative. The object corresponds to the many embodiments of redemption in the Christian narrative (eschatology, doctrines of redemption, grace).

4. The subject. The hero or protagonist in the narrative. The subject corresponds to both symbolizations of Christ (in the original narrative) and the individual or community (we, us) as well in the broader Christian narrative (Christology, soteriology, doctrines of calling, conversion, faith, justification, sanctification, perseverance).

5. The helper. The donor or enabler in the narrative, without whose help the hero would not be able to attain the object. In the original Christian narrative, it would include all symbolizations of the power or Spirit of God. In the broader Christian paradigm (since, in classical terminology, the ascension of Christ), this role includes symbolizations of Christ and the Spirit of Christ, the church, the sacraments, the Bible, and the minister (pneumatology, Christology, ecclesiology, sacramental theology, doctrines of Scripture, ordination).

6. The opponent. The villain or false hero who impedes the efforts of the subject. This actant corresponds to all symbolic embodiments of sin and evil in the Christian narrative structure (doctrines of sin and evil, the Fall, temptation).[9]

9. The above is adapted from Robert Scholes, *Structuralism in Literature: An Introduction* (New Haven: Yale University Press, 1978), 105–6. See A. J. Gremais, *Semantique structurale* (Paris: Larousse, 1966); Étienne Souriau, *Les deux cent mille situations dramatiques* (Paris: Flammarion, 1950); and Vladimir Propp, *Morphology of the Folktale* (Austin: University of Texas Press, 1970).

FIGURE 1
Actantial Model

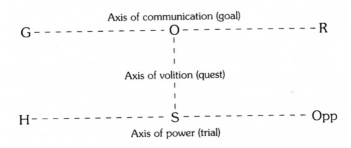

Gremais's structure[10] can be visualized as shown in Figure 1.[11] The content of the theosymbolic code in preaching is the collection of typical roles each of these characters plays in the narrative structure embedded in a preacher's sermons.

The easiest way to discern these typical roles is to look for them in the results of your idea inventory. In other words, look for these roles as they are embedded in your fundamental semantic lexicon. For example, a preacher named Dan, after performing an idea inventory on two years of his sermons, determined that his basic semantic lexicon (or seven, plus or minus two, ideas) was as shown in Table 6.

Placing Gremais's narrative theological structure over his lexicon as a grid, Dan determined the basic outline of his theosymbolic content (Figure 2, p. 99).

This short process for determining theosymbolic content can and should be lengthened and made more detailed. To do so, label six sheets of paper Giver, Receiver, Object, Helper, Subject, and Opponent. Then go back through your sermons for the past year or so and jot down on these sheets of paper the various roles or qualities you attribute to each of these "characters" or actants. (See the concluding chapter for an example of this kind of sermon decoding.) Then,

---

10. For further explanation of each axis, see Patte, *What Is Structural Exegesis?* 42–43.
11. John Dominic Crossan adapts the terminology "axis of communication," "axis of volition," and "axis of trial" from Roland Barthes. See Crossan, *The Dark Interval: Toward a Theology of Story* (Niles, Ill.: Argus Communications, 1975), 65.

TABLE 6
Dan's Idea Inventory

Subject	*Basic Meaning*
Witness	Witness is absolutely necessary to be a Christian.
Faith	Faith is risky.
Faith	Faith is demanding.
Knowledge of God	God is known through our experience of God.
Church	The church is Christ's presence in the world.
Church	The church has a tremendous responsibility.
Transformation	Transformation comes when we encounter God.
Service	Service of God is service of others.
Christ's presence	Christ's presence is known in times of crisis.

FIGURE 2
Dan's Theosymbolic Structure

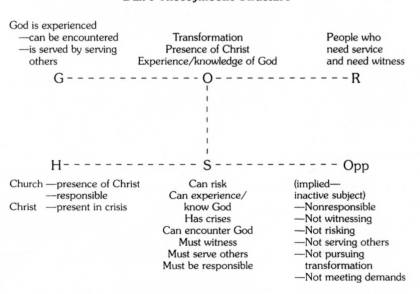

on each page, group each role into categories until you have determined the basic variants that exist for each character. This longer process is more precise in determining the relative strength with which a particular character or actant is represented in your preaching. In other words, this process shows you precisely how many times you spoke of God, Christ, the church, evil, the world, and so on in your preaching. It is also helpful in determining how well and in what ways each character or actant is developed in your theosymbolic structure.

Three questions should be asked of each actant in your narrative structure in order to determine how this theosymbolic content affects your theosymbolic style. First of all, is an actant strong or weak? Strong actants are not abstractions we are told something about; they are realities we are shown, that are concretely embodied, or who actually speak and act in certain ways in your preaching. For instance, in Dan's theosymbolic structure or faith story, the helper is weakly characterized as long as Dan abstractly calls it the "presence of Christ." As Dan turns this presence into a powerful manifestation and shows us in concrete images a rich portrait of Christ who is present and whose presence says and means specific things to us, this actant becomes stronger. E. M. Forster reminds us that strong characters are "round" characters; unlike "flat" and "stock" characters, they possess a wider variety of traits and are less predictable.[12]

Second, does an actant occur frequently or infrequently in your preaching? The more frequently an actant appears, the more significant and powerful this actant is in your larger theosymbolic structure. If the helper shows up in your preaching only occasionally, then we conclude that the helper is not a significant or strong character in your theosymbolic structure.

Third, what fundamental kinds of relationships exist between the characters or actants? Is the helper identified closely with the giver? With the subject? Is the opponent only a foil for the object? Is the opponent used to obscure the object? Is the receiver similar to the

---

12. E. M. Forster, *Aspects of the Novel* (New York: Harcourt, Brace & World, 1954), 103–18. See also M. H. Abrams, *A Glossary of Literary Terms*, 4th ed. (New York: Holt, Rinehart & Winston, 1981), 185; and Jack Dean Kingsbury, *Matthew as Story*, 2d ed. (Philadelphia: Fortress Press, 1988), 9–10.

subject or very different? Does the giver confront the opponent directly or only through other characters such as helper or subject? Look closely at all relationships and take note of them.

As you do this content analysis and answer these questions, you will start to become aware of the kind of faith story you are telling your congregation. With this information in hand, you can begin to determine your theosymbolic style and the kind of theological worldview you are sponsoring in your preaching.

INTERTEXT OF WORLDVIEW

The theosymbolic code in preaching sponsors what Geertz calls "world view."[13] According to Geertz *worldview* is the "picture" a community shares "of the way things in sheer actuality are," a community's "most comprehensive ideas of order."[14] According to James Hopewell, who makes use of the Geertz definition of worldview in *Congregation: Stories and Structures,* a religious community "over time develops a shared sense of what is really going on in the world."[15] Geertz illustrates how religious communities formulate "by means of symbols, . . . an image of . . . a genuine order of the world which will account for, even celebrate, the perceived ambiguities, puzzles and paradoxes of human experience."[16]

According to Geertz, the relation between worldview and ethos is integral and inseparable. Whereas worldview is principally the "cognitive, existential" aspects of a community's reality picture, ethos includes "evaluative elements" such as "tone, character, and quality

---

13. Geertz, *The Interpretation of Cultures,* 127.
14. Ibid. See also James Hopewell, *Congregation: Stories and Structures* (Philadelphia: Fortress Press, 1987).
15. Hopewell, *Congregation: Stories and Structures,* 55. James Hopewell's book is an attempt to sort out four types of congregational worldviews—gnostic, charismatic, canonic, and empiric—based upon the four archetypal *mythoi*—romance, comedy, tragedy, and irony—proposed by Northrop Frye in his landmark book, *Anatomy of Criticism* (Princeton: Princeton University Press, 1957), 71–239. Because the narrative approach we are using is more structuralist than archetypalist, we will not find Hopewell's and Frye's categories to be a perfect fit with the worldview types we will see being sponsored in preaching. The significant overlaps will be noted along the way.
16. Quoted in Hopewell, 56.

of life, . . . moral and aesthetic style and mood; . . . the underlying attitude" a community has "toward themselves and their world."[17]

The way a preacher uses and patterns the basic symbols of the Christian faith sponsors a theological worldview and its accompanying ethos in a congregation. In other words, the way a preacher relates sin and redemption, God and humanity, Christ and the individual, or evil and the individual contributes substantially to the community's comprehensive reality picture. In the remainder of this chapter we will investigate the different ways preachers tend to pattern the basic symbols of the Christian faith (theosymbolic styles) and the corresponding kinds of theological worldviews supported by each of these styles.

Before moving on, however, we need to ask whether preaching contributes anything distinctive to the shaping of the language-shaped reality or "intertext" of worldview in the church. Once again, we need to note that preaching relates theological worldviews to Scripture. If a preacher is sponsoring a particular theological worldview, that worldview must be related to the biblical witness in his or her preaching. This worldview will, of course, have hermeneutical implications for the preacher. The same text may be interpreted in a variety of ways, depending upon the preacher's theosymbolic style and worldview. Likewise, some texts will be avoided because of difficulties in making them fit the preacher's dominant theosymbolic style and worldview. No matter what worldview is promoted, however, the biblical content introduces certain constraints and limits beyond which the preacher cannot proceed. In preaching, worldviews are not only authorized and defended through interaction with the biblical text but also sometimes explored, critiqued, and changed through that interaction.

STYLES

As we have already indicated, the theosymbolic code in preaching sponsors (vouches for, promotes, and responds to) the intertext of worldview in the church. Let us now look at how theological symbols

---

17. Geertz, *The Interpretation of Cultures,* 126–27. See also Wesley Kort, *Narrative Elements and Religious Meaning* (Philadelphia: Fortress Press, 1975), 20–39. What Kort defines as narrative "atmosphere" is similar to Geertz's idea of cultural ethos.

are encoded in preaching and how the different styles sponsor theological worldviews in congregations.

Vouching for the Intertext

Theological worldviews are vouched for when preachers consciously activate and interrelate the major characters of the Christian story, when preachers intentionally encode symbolizations of God, Christ, church, humanity, the individual, world, evil, and redemption in their preaching as dynamic, interrelated characters in an energized, ongoing faith story. As we have already suggested, theological ideas are not isolated from one another. They are not solitary concepts, hypotheses, or metaphors that exist on their own as objects of reflection. Whether intentionally or unintentionally, they are integrated in sermons as parts of a larger story and vision. When a concept such as "sin is hiding" is preached, it takes a role in a larger theological structure of faith story that is present in the preacher's rhetoric.

We have already suggested that the idea that "sin is hiding" could appear in the homiletical faith story as a devilish opponent, powerful and pervasive, meeting us at every turn and throwing us back on our own resources or on our need for a helper constantly. Quite differently, this idea could appear as a smaller, less powerful opponent that has already been confronted and limited in its power by the large and powerful reality of Christ in the community. Instead of being thrown back on our own resources or need for a helper, we are told that we are free as Christians to live out in the open and invite others to come out of hiding and into a similar life of full partnership. When preachers intentionally and consistently place theological symbols in dynamic roles in a larger theological structure, people are most effectively oriented toward those symbols in a particular way. Hiding can be used intentionally to make sin more powerful and pervasive in the structure, or it can be used intentionally to make sin into a foil to set off the more powerful redemptive work of Christ, who "brings people out of hiding." In either case, people are invited into a larger theological story and vision in which the sin of hiding plays a particular role. When this happens, preaching vouches for a theological worldview in the congregation. It says "this is our worldview" or "this is the way we see sin in relation to everything else."

Perhaps the most common problem that can weaken the theosymbolic code in preaching is inconsistency. The effect of inconsistency is similar to the effect of reading a novel in which the plot and all of the relationships between the basic characters suddenly and completely change, with no warning. In preaching, theosymbolic inconsistency occurs when two different theosymbolic styles coexist and compete in the preaching of a single preacher or, in a multiple-staff situation, between preachers. For instance, if the two visions of the role of sin that we have just elaborated are juxtaposed over and over again in a preacher's sermons, one tends to undermine the other, and a weakly "vouched for" worldview comes from the pulpit.

The key to the strength of the theosymbolic code is to work for focus, depth, and consistency in the roles that are taken for each symbolic character or actant in the larger theological structure embedded in your preaching. If you are able to do this, your preaching will vouch strongly for a particular worldview in the preaching of the church.

Promoting the Intertext

Each of the five fundamental theosymbolic styles in preaching directly or indirectly promotes a similar theological worldview in the community. The five styles consist of two larger categories of style, negative and positive, a high and low substyle in each larger category, and a reversal style.[18]

Negative Style

In order to understand what is meant by a negative style, we must look again at the structural outline (Figure 3). Added to the outline in Figure 1 are plus (+) and minus (–) signs. Negative styles are those that accentuate the minus side of the narrative structure. In these styles the opponent and receiver are symbolized with greater consis-

---

18. These five ways, as will be seen, are based upon the structural analysis of myth and folktale. See Claude Lévi-Strauss, *The Savage Mind* (Chicago: University of Chicago Press, 1968); *Structural Anthropology* (London: Penguin Books, 1972); E. Kögas Maranda and Pierre Maranda, *Structural Models in Folklore and Transformational Essays* (The Hague: Mouton, 1971); and John Dominic Crossan, *The Dark Interval.*

FIGURE 3
Model of Negative and Positive Styles

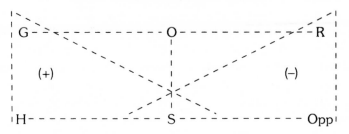

tency, strength, and depth in relationship to the subject than are the helper and giver.

The negative style promotes a worldview of *lack*.[19] It promotes a congregational worldview in which something is missing, not right, in need, deficient, in a state of paradox, inconsistent, irregular, or double-bound. It is a worldview in which reality is marked by antithesis.

Low-Negative Style

This theosymbolic style creates a faith story with an opposition or problem (lack) but "no mediator"[20] to set things right. In the low-negative style the opponent is assumed and defined, but not engaged. Neither the helper nor the subject enters into active "battle" with the opponent in preaching. This engagement or battle remains a possibility or hypothesis. It may be supposed to happen, but it is not happening in the preaching itself. It may be encouraged from time to time,

---

19. For various permutations of this concept of lack, see Jacques Lacan, *Écrits: A Selection*, trans. Alan Sheridan (New York: W. W. Norton, 1977); L. J. Kalinich, "The Logos in Lacan," *St. Vladimir's Quarterly* 32 (1988), 367–83; Crossan, *The Dark Interval*, 51–53; Anthony Wilden, *System and Structure: Essays in Communication and Exchange* (London: Tavistock Publications, 1972), 2–30; Rosiland Coward and John Ellis, *Language and Materialism: Developments in Semiology and the Theory of the Subject* (London: Routledge & Kegan Paul, 1977), 108–20; M. Merleau-Ponty, *Phenomenology of Perception* (London: Routledge & Kegan Paul), 183; Jacques Derrida, *Positions*, trans. Alan Bass (Chicago: University of Chicago Press, 1981), 29; and Paul Watzlawick, Janet Helmut Beavin, and Don D. Jackson, *Pragmatics of Human Communication: A Study of Interactional Patterns, Pathologies and Paradoxes* (New York: W. W. Norton, 1967), 257–71.

20. See Maranda and Maranda, *Structural Models*, 36; and Crossan, *The Dark Interval*, 52.

on the outside, beyond the text, beyond the sermon, but it is not an active, present process in preaching. The subject does not submit to the opponent; instead, it avoids, endures, or accepts the opponent as an uncomfortable, difficult, but inevitable part of the order of things. The helper is not presented as a powerful, exciting character but rather as more of a companion character, consoler, support, or guide. The giver is present and available but is not an independent, active, engaged character with unique attributes or powers in the story.

Structurally the object is beyond the narrative. It is what the receiver continues to lack. The faith story ends in a state of unresolved tension or lack. This final state of lack, however, is sometimes given the semantic face of an object to be desired: the Stoic mask, self-acceptance and maturity (from some types of psychotherapy), solidarity with the oppressed, empathy, compassion, some forms of community, honesty, endurance, awareness of the presence of God or Christ, a sense of irony, or even Promethean defiance. All of these ideas easily fall within the semantic domain of this object. The only object within the low-negative narrative structure, then, is the state of unresolved lack, a state that could be made to mean many different things.[21]

In Dan's semantic lexicon and theosymbolic structure (Fig. 2), this low-negative theosymbolic style appears to be dominant. The opponent in Dan's theosymbolic structure, although largely implied, is concrete, pervasive, and strong. It is the congregation itself, characterized as those who lack responsibility, fail to witness, seldom take risks, do not serve others, need transformation, and fail to meet God's expectations. The subject's engagement with the opponent is encouraged but not actually accomplished in the preaching of the sermon; the subject can risk, can experience God, can know God's presence

---

21. James Hopewell's semantic categories of thought for the empiric worldview are also suggestive for the low-negative style. He suggests "love," "community," and "regularity" as objects within this worldview. In response to Hopewell's more archetypalist (and therefore content-centered) approach, however, semantic categories do not define worldview style; their use, place, or role in the theosymbolic structure defines the style. For instance, acceptance, honesty, endurance, love, community, and regularity could all be qualities of the subject engaged in a heroic quest rather than objects pursued. This would dramatically change the structure and accompanying worldview and ethos.

in crises, can encounter God, must witness, must serve others, and must be responsible, but is not actually placed in these situations in sermons. The helper is present or a presence but not a strong, active figure. God is experienced and can be encountered and served but is not independent and active as a concrete character in Dan's theosymbolic structure. The object is "the presence of Christ" and the "experience/knowledge of God," objects that do not function strongly to resolve any of the lacks that are introduced.

In Dan's sermon on the Mary and Martha text, we might expect him to teach, inform, or make people aware of the sin of hiding. Although he may encourage or imply some active confrontation with the sin of hiding, he will not, in his preaching, bring his hearers into an immediate confrontation with this villain. He will acknowledge its reality and force in human experience. His sermon will tell people, in essence, to be aware of the sin of hiding and to beware of its pervasive grip on their lives. The congregation may see in Christ the one who first made us aware of this sin and is present with us as we come to grips with it. As mature Christians we can be in solidarity with those who have been forced into hiding. We, like them, must learn to endure in the face of this problem. We are aware that God in Christ is present with us in the midst of this situation as a consolation and support.

CONSIDERATIONS

The low-negative theosymbolic style in preaching sponsors a *tensive* worldview in the church. People are invited to see reality as filled with paradoxes and problems that might be defined and categorized but that can never be resolved. The church is sometimes characterized as a community that recognizes, accepts, and endures together particular forms of existential or social tension. No matter how the community is characterized, however, unresolved tension dominates the preacher's picture of the way things really are.

One problem with the low-negative theosymbolic style is that when it is used unconsciously it can communicate pessimism, lack of conviction, or theological insecurity. The unconscious tensivist unwittingly avoids providing any theological clue to the resolution of the tensive nature of reality. For the unconscious tensivist, for instance, like Dan, the preacher's personal convictions regarding the plus actants (giver and helper) may be at loose ends. He is not as sure as he once was about what he believes about God, Christ, the church, or the Bible. Therefore, he is undecided about the relative power of the helper and giver in his homiletical faith story. The result is that he has leveled sin and evil to a set of manageable and uneventful moral failures in his congregation. His avoidance of powerful, disrupting opponents enables him to avoid having to search for more powerful characterizations of the giver and helper. This approach leads to a flat and lifeless homiletical faith story that can communicate lack of theological conviction and energy or a creeping pessimism.

The only solution to this problem for the preacher with a low-negative style is to strive to become more certain about what he or she does believe, no matter how reduced or minimal these beliefs may be. Then the preacher's low-negative theosymbolic style will not be so by default, but by intention. It will fit the preacher's overall convictional, theological, and pastoral strategy.

Another problem with the low-negative style is that sometimes the intense, committed tensivist develops defensive, dogmatic strategies that can reshape the low-negative style into a kind of absurdist faith story. For the intentional, committed, theological tensivist, images of potential or partial resolution are consolationist, demonstrating an inability to accept or endure the fundamental paradoxes of life and an easy way out. The conscious tensivist can get into the habit of rigorously and suspiciously limiting the power of all potential mediators in the narration of the Christian faith story so that a worldview of tensivity might be maintained. The narrative force and influence of God, Christ, church, and Bible are carefully pared down to a minimum. Going still further, the doctrinaire tensivist can devote constant effort to limiting the power of individuals or communities (subjects) in the faith story who might attempt to alter or resolve the basic paradoxes or problems of life. The preacher is convinced that these individuals or communities typically develop fantastic hero or martyr complexes, unrealistic or self-destructive pictures of the powers of the human subject in the face of inexorable existential and spiritual tension. When these kinds of character levelings occur habitually and incessantly, the plot for the homiletical faith story can become defiant and even cruel, or it can represent a kind of absurdism that is needlessly reductionistic to those who draw upon broader dimensions of reality and experience in their understanding of the Christian faith story.

This problem is partially overcome by emphasizing the more energized and constructive semantic faces that unresolved tension can have. Rather than protecting a tensive worldview by weakening certain characterizations in the theosymbolic structure, the preacher concentrates on establishing tensivity in a candid and forthright way that invests affirmative energy in recognizing and embracing unresolved tension. In this way, the preacher avoids turning irony and paradox into satire and absurdity.[22]

In the Mary and Martha sermon, for instance, the preacher does not have to be chronically worried about rooting out all attempts to elevate Christ to superhuman status in the story or about making sure that the congregation knows in no uncertain terms that they can ultimately do nothing, even with the help of Christ, to overcome the impact of hiding in their own lives. Instead, the preacher can focus on the awareness of the sin of hiding as a reality in our own lives and on the presence of Christ, who deepens that awareness and is in solidarity with us as we endure its impact.

The strength of the low-negative style is its celebration of authenticity and honesty. The good news is embedded not in the sublime, the beautiful, or the heroic, but in the authentic.[23] People are invited not to discover the good news by assuming fantastic religious roles in profound religious plots but to find the traces of good news in authentic existence, stripped of all but the most self-congruent roles and devoid of plot developments that would promote faulty images of either self or the world in which we live. Little that is sentimental, fantastic, or pretentious is in this style or in the tensive worldview it promotes. This theosymbolic style and worldview can be a healthy development in a congregation that has been enmeshed in a highly fanciful and fabulous Christian worldview that has bred an inauthentic or even delusive vision of reality.

22. For more on the distinctions among irony, satire, picaresque, and absurdist forms of narrative, see Scholes, *Structuralism in Literature,* 120–23. For an excellent study of the way in which faith "imagines" an ironic worldview, see William F. Lynch, S.J., *Images of Faith: An Exploration of the Ironic Imagination* (Notre Dame, Ind.: University of Notre Dame Press, 1973).

23. Lionel Trilling, *Sincerity and Authenticity* (London: Oxford University Press, 1974), 81–106.

NEGOTIATING A HEARING

This style sometimes corresponds to the theological worldview of those who have been through counseling or psychotherapy, to those who are intellectual realists, and to those who have been disillusioned with the consolationism or cheap grace of some forms of Christianity. For many, however, this style of preaching is heard as full-blown "secular humanism" or as atheism, because it avoids or denies the forms of mediation that many assume to be the central message of the gospel.

In order to negotiate a hearing, the preacher must be careful not to adopt a negative, judgmental posture toward competing worldviews, especially those that accentuate the redemptive rather than the tensive aspects of the Christian faith story. Lampooning or satirizing other worldviews as religious fantasies or delusions does not help. The preacher in the initial stages of negotiating a hearing may want to do exactly the opposite, showing that the recovery of the authentic and the tensive does not necessarily preclude mediation or resolution but simply acknowledges that this dimension is beyond the story *we* can authentically tell, beyond what we can say and still be true to the reality of human existence. This approach amounts to a bracketing of mediation rather than an actual denial of its existence. This bracketing is done not for the negative purpose of crusading against other worldviews but for the positive reason of recovering authenticity and actuality in the way that Christians envision reality.

High-Negative Style

This theosymbolic style creates a faith story with an opposition or problem (lack) that is actively engaged but in which "mediation fails" or is failing.[24] *Failing* means simply that the resolution of narrative tension is pursued and only partially achieved. Narrative mediation is attempted but is not adequate to the depth and breadth of narrative lack. In this style, the opponent is engaged in serious and prolonged battle. Both the helper and the subject are characterized in

---

24. See Maranda and Maranda, *Structural Models,* 36; and Crossan, *The Dark Interval,* 52.

sermons as engaged with this opponent in some crucial and critical encounter. The subject is not only aware of the opponent but also committed to its eventual destruction. The helper is strong but not strong enough for an immediate and total victory over the opponent. The subject is more active and involved in moving with strength along the axis of volition toward the object. The giver is independent and strong but remote, lost behind the looming image of the opponent, and waiting on the other side of the conflict. The giver enters the conflict with the opponent but only indirectly through other characters, in ways that decrease the giver's objective power in the theosymbolic structure. The power of the giver is dependent on others in the narrative structure. In other words, spiritual warfare is not fought in the sky with human subjects contributing prayers and offerings. It is fought in the arenas of history and human experience, with God contributing self-commitments, promises, and priests for the process.

The object is not narratively framed as what the receiver lacks but as what the subject wills. It is the object of a quest; it is what the subject wants or desires but only partially receives. This object reflects a structural state of partial resolution. Minor victories provide a glimpse of eventual major defeat. Semantic faces for this object include such things as hope, forgiveness, getting saved, justification, kingdom, judgment, courage, and "living in the promises." Again, these are simply diverse meanings that are sometimes given to the structural state of partial resolution.

Another case, that of Barbara, illustrates this high-negative style. Barbara's theosymbolic structure looks like Figure 4. In Barbara's theosymbolic structure, the opponent is pervasive and strong but is engaged in battle on the field of history by a subject who is willing to resist, work for peace, and suffer. The helper is figured as Christ, church, and Scripture. Christ has gone before and established a pattern of suffering love and of "strange" or type-contradictory heroic actions, which continue in the church. Scripture helps by promising and suggesting a future that contradicts the evil of this present age. The giver is "the power of the future" who waits on the other side of the conflict. The giver enters the conflict by giving up all power and suffering through the actions of the subject and helper. The object is a state of partial resolution: various releases from dehumanization, experiences of forgiveness, and a sense of hope in history.

FIGURE 4
Barbara's Theosymbolic Structure

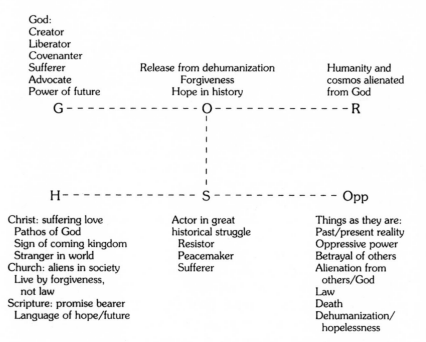

God:
Creator
Liberator
Covenanter
Sufferer   Release from dehumanization   Humanity and
Advocate   Forgiveness   cosmos alienated
Power of future   Hope in history   from God

G - - - - - - - - - - - - - O - - - - - - - - - - - - R
                            |
                            |
                            |
                            |
                            |
                            |
H - - - - - - - - - - - - - S - - - - - - - - - - - Opp

Christ: suffering love   Actor in great   Things as they are:
  Pathos of God   historical struggle   Past/present reality
  Sign of coming kingdom   Resistor   Oppressive power
  Stranger in world   Peacemaker   Betrayal of others
Church: aliens in society   Sufferer   Alienation from
  Live by forgiveness,   others/God
    not law   Law
Scripture: promise bearer   Death
  Language of hope/future   Dehumanization/
                                                           hopelessness

In Barbara's Mary and Martha sermon, the sin of hiding is a large and formidable opponent. Instead of making people aware of the sin of hiding and encouraging them to accept and endure it in ways that deflect its negative impact, Barbara engages this opponent in the sermon. The sermon carries a mood of confrontation, a sense that now is the time for battle. Instead of communicating "we can live with that," the sermon communicates "we are overcoming that." We do not acknowledge and endure the sin of hiding; we confront it. Empowered by the promises of Scripture and the pattern of Christ that identifies God with its struggle, the community plunges into the midst of this conflict; they are prepared to suffer as they confront their own hiding and their own complicity in patterns of life that force some persons into hiding. Only when this occurs can the community achieve partial victories that show that God's promises are trustworthy and that God will one day resolve this conflict and hiding (sin) will be no more.

CONSIDERATIONS

The high-negative theosymbolic style in preaching promotes an *oppositional* worldview.[25] What was unengaged tension in the low-negative style becomes engaged opposition in this style. The congregation may be characterized as a community that recognizes, confronts, and suffers together in their confrontation with the sin and evil that threatens both the individual and the community. Being involved now, in the very moment of preaching, in confronting the opponent and in willing (desiring, struggling for, pursuing) something else is important. No matter what the semantic content of this structure is, the vision of an object willed but not yet received—the vision of partial resolution—dominates the preacher's picture of the way things really are.

One problem with the high-negative theosymbolic style is that it can degenerate into a form of moralism. What appears as simple tension, light and dark, in the low-negative style is in the high-negative style imbued with forceful positive and negative values and becomes opposition: two forces, one good, the other evil, confronting each other. As the individual and community form alliances with the good and make decisions to confront the evil, the preacher's faith story can easily reify these decisions (about what is good and evil) and construct a moral system. Then, support of this moral system becomes the principal reason to perpetuate an oppositional worldview through preaching. This process further obscures the partially realized object of the high-negative faith story, which is, paradoxically, freedom from opposition or moral tension altogether, a mode of being in which opposition is resolved, "All things are lawful," and "nothing is impure," to quote the apostle Paul.[26]

The best way to overcome this problem is for the preacher to

25. Again, depending on the semantic content the preacher puts into this structure, it may resemble some aspects of Frye's "tragic" mythoi and James Hopewell's "canonic" worldview.
26. For an excellent essay on this subtle kind of moralism, see Jacques Ellul, *The Subversion of Christianity*, trans. Geoffrey Bromiley (Grand Rapids: Wm. B. Eerdmans, 1986), 69–94.

accentuate the subject's desire for the object as the larger framework for the battle with various opponents. The preacher's faith story should always present the battle with opponents as a part of a larger quest rather than as an end in itself. In the Mary and Martha sermon, for instance, the sin of hiding does not simply provide us with an opportunity to put on our hero hats and make another charge at the forces of evil for the sake of doing and representing the forces of good. Rather, the sin of hiding is another obstacle that obscures the crucial but partial vision of promised freedom from hiding and all forms of sin in human life.

Another problem with this style is that it can promote a communal martyr complex, a negative focus on heroic sacrifice for its own sake. This occurs because failing mediation is at the heart of this theosymbolic model. Like the thirty frescoes of Pomarancio in the church of the German Hungarian College, Santo Stefano Rotondo, with their lurid anatomical scenes of the severed limbs of dismembered saints, the high-negative faith story can venerate sacrificial heroism in a way that obscures the role of sacrifice in the larger Christian faith story. Intensity of desire, extent of volition, and radicality of action can readily be celebrated for their own sake or in order to inspire commitment. [27] Christian sacrifice, however, is not an end in itself, a tool to persuade believers to sacrificial service, or a means of self-exoneration. It is something that sometimes occurs when Christians are true to their calling and serious in their confrontation with the power of sin and evil in this world. Again, the best way to overcome this problem is to place more emphasis on partial mediation than on failed mediation. Accentuate the partial vision of resolution in the faith story so that failure does not become a dominant motif.

The strength of the high-negative style is its focus on immediate, present narrative action. The good news of Jesus Christ is discovered

---

27. Martyrdom art was popular during the reform eras of the sixteenth century and was used principally for training and inspiring young Jesuits to sacrificial service. During the pre-Constantinian period, however, when persecutions and martyrdoms were common, the art on the catacomb walls rarely depicted martyrdom, and even then, according to Margaret Miles, "the mood is consistently peaceful" (*Image as Insight: Visual Understanding in Western Christianity and Secular Culture* [Boston: Beacon Press, 1985], 47, 122).

in the midst of decisive, committed, expectant action. Congregations are invited to embark immediately on a quest or journey toward something special, unique, and already partially active in their lives. This theosymbolic style and worldview can be especially beneficial in a congregation that has settled into inactivity, either as the result of having adopted a consolationist vision that God will work everything out for the best or as the result of having opted for an absurdist tensivist vision in which what we do does not really matter anyway because it will not make any difference.

NEGOTIATING A HEARING

For the person with a tensive worldview, the oppositional world-view can easily represent a movement away from authenticity toward roles that are fantastic and out of proportion. Such people see as ill-advised the characterization of human subjects as capable of realizing some form of resolution, no matter how partial or fragmentary, to the basic tensivity of human existence. This style could easily slip into full-blown consolationism and delusion.

To negotiate a hearing for the oppositional worldview with the tensivist, the oppositionalist must clearly indicate the partiality of the resolution that motivates the oppositionalist vision. Without denying the reality and power of this inspiring vision of resolution, the oppositionalist must clearly acknowledge that it is not fully understood or received, even when confrontations with sin and evil have proven highly successful. The oppositionalist must also be careful not to elevate the human subject to superhuman heroic stature. Following the lead of the Bible, as opposed to Greek tragedy, the preacher must accentuate the human ordinariness of the subject who enters actively into the historical project of willing and journeying toward the promised object.[28]

For those who are expecting to hear more resolution and victory in the confrontation with the opponent in the Christian faith story, the oppositionalist will want to accentuate the convictional certitude

---

28. See Erich Auerbach, *Mimesis: The Representation of Reality in Western Literature,* trans. Willard R. Trask (Princeton: Princeton University Press, 1953), 22, for further elaboration on this distinction between Greek tragedy and the tragic dimensions of biblical narrative.

inspired by the object in the faith story. Sermons will concentrate on the vision of partial resolution as an inspiring guarantee that resolution and victory are on the horizon for the Christian. In this way, the oppositionalist moves as close as possible to those for whom some sense of resolution is very important to the Christian vision.

Positive Style

Positive styles accentuate the plus side of the narrative structure. They are styles in which the giver and helper are symbolized with greater consistency, strength, and depth in relation to the subject than are receiver and opponent.

Positive style promotes a worldview of *plenitude*. It promotes a congregational worldview in which something has been accomplished already, something has been fulfilled, and something has been established, restored, or made whole. It is a worldview marked by the mediation of tension and opposition.

Low-Positive Style

The theosymbolic style creates a faith story in which a "successful mediation" "nullifies the impact" of the story's central problem or lack.[29] In the low-positive style the opponent has insufficient power to disrupt constantly an assumed order of reality. Although the opponent disturbs this order, the impact of this disturbance is nullified by the stronger and more profound actions of the helper on behalf of the subject. Despite any "bad news," the "good news" always counterbalances and restores equilibrium. Confrontation with the opponent is serious but not prolonged. The subject acts in confidence that adequate help is available and present to overcome any difficulty. Helper and giver emerge as independent characters with unique powers of their own. The helper is characterized as adequate in the immediate situation to keep the opponent from making any significant or permanent impact. The helper has special unique powers that bring about a positive resolution to the disruption brought by the opponent. The giver emerges from behind the noise and disruption

---

29. See Maranda and Maranda, *Structural Models,* 36; and Crossan, *The Dark Interval,* 52.

of confrontation with the opponent and is present as the one who is now giving the anticipated object to the receiver.

The object is not characterized as what the receiver lacks or as what the subject desires but as what *the giver has been attempting to communicate all along and is now able to give freely.* The object reflects a structural state of restored equilibrium. When equilibrium is present, the giver can communicate freely what is necessary for the receiver. No longer is the process of communication between giver and receiver significantly blocked. The pathway between them is clear. Semantic faces for this object vary: peace, harmony, union,[30] reconciliation, enlightenment, order, wholeness, integration, new life, transformation, and salvation are possibilities. Again, these are simply diverse meanings that are sometimes attributed to the structural state of restored equilibrium.

The case of Bob illustrates this low-positive style. Bob's theosymbolic structure looks like Figure 5. In Bob's theosymbolic structure the opponent is easily identified and restrained in its power to disrupt the equilibrium of the overall structure. Many people do not know of the reconciliation offered by God in Christ and fail to participate in it, but this failure does not significantly impede the reception of that reconciliation by "those who trust Jesus Christ." The greatest strength in the theosymbolic structure is attributed to the helper: Christ as Lord, Savior, Redeemer, and Son of God and the church as the redeemed community, who are characterized as centered in Scripture as God's Word and as having a strong, positive ministry of witness, sharing, and testimony. The community and individual believers are not characterized as subjects doing perpetual battle with an overpowering opponent but as harbingers of the reality of the object: wholeness, reconciliation, and joy. God is not glimpsed through the dust and debris of confrontation with an opponent but is approached as "Lord of my life," as the one who has given and is still giving reconciliation, wholeness, and peace to individuals, just as the proper order of things requires. The negative impact of the opponent is

---

30. These first three reflect Hopewell's interpretation of this structural model as primarily "gnostic" in content, although, again, this is only one possible interpretation of this worldview (*Congregation: Stories and Structures,* 70).

FIGURE 5
Bob's Theosymbolic Structure

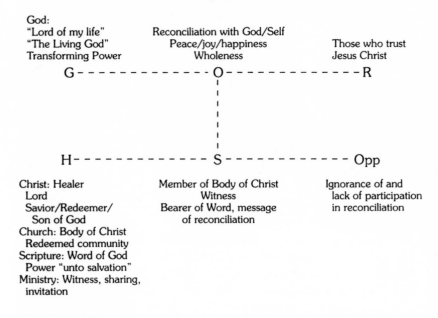

God:
"Lord of my life"   Reconciliation with God/Self
"The Living God"   Peace/joy/happiness   Those who trust
Transforming Power   Wholeness   Jesus Christ

G – – – – – – – – – – – – – O – – – – – – – – – – – – R

H – – – – – – – – – – – – S – – – – – – – – – – – – Opp

Christ: Healer   Member of Body of Christ   Ignorance of and
Lord   Witness   lack of participation
Savior/Redeemer/   Bearer of Word, message   in reconciliation
Son of God   of reconciliation
Church: Body of Christ
Redeemed community
Scripture: Word of God
Power "unto salvation"
Ministry: Witness, sharing,
invitation

nullified by this state of affairs, and congregational worldview is focused on a state of restored equilibrium and unimpeded communication between giver and receiver.

Bob preaches his sermon on the Mary and Martha text with little focus on the hidden negative in the text. Bob accentuates the presence of Jesus Christ and his redemptive power in the lives of both women and in our lives. The sermon carries a mood of resolution. Instead of engendering confrontation with the sin of hiding, Christ's actions resolve, heal, and bring wholeness where hiding once existed. Instead of communicating "we can live with that" or "we are overcoming that," the sermon communicates that "we have overcome that." God is already communicating new life in the present moment: freedom from hiding, healing for the wounds caused by hiding, and a sense of joy and peace that comes from the restoration of wholeness in our lives.

CONSIDERATIONS

No matter what the semantic content of the theosymbolic structure, the low-positive theosymbolic style in preaching promotes an
equilibrational worldview.[31] Tension and opposition (elements
expressing lack) are there but are ultimately not strongly disruptive
features in this style. The congregation is sometimes characterized as
a community that, by virtue of identification with a strong, tested,
and capable helper, is able to experience and share in a life of relative stability and balance, receive God's grace in due measure, and
become enablers of that grace in the lives of others. The stable vision
of an object communicated and received dominates the preacher's
picture of the way things really are.

The basic problem with the low-positive theosymbolic style is that
it can easily become a monotonous status quo rhetoric. It can develop
into a repetitive, cyclical style that predictably returns the congregation to the same happy point of departure with no significant gains or
losses, only the same familiar, consoling sense that order prevails and
everything is fine. Congregations who are used to this style know
that no matter how confrontational and disruptive the gospel might
be, its message always has some restoration and some constitutive
dimension for us. They know that no matter how bad human sin and
the forces of evil may become, we can be confident that some form
of modest redemption can be found that will have the final word.

Not only are negative excesses brought under control in this style
but also positive excesses are checked carefully as well. Redemption
is not something that produces a whole new reality, an event or process that leaves us gasping for breath, half terrified and half desperate for its next expressive impact on our lives. Rather, redemption
restores and consoles; we rejoice in it but with controlled joy and an
attitude of measured contentment and relief.

The preacher in this style needs to be attentive to the potential
loss of energy that comes naturally with a style that is supportive of a
worldview of equilibrium. Because of its fundamental investment in

---

31. Depending on the semantic content the preacher puts into this structure, it may
resemble some aspects of Frye's comic mythoi and James Hopewell's gnostic worldview. As the case of Bob illustrates, however, the more structural approach to worldview permits far more variety of content while allowing for a low-positive worldview.

the restoration and perpetuation of order, this style can easily degenerate into a maintenance rhetoric for the status quo, a soft-sell religion for those who want only to be soothed.

The best way to overcome this problem is to redefine the status quo periodically and reconsider what equilibrium is so that it does not become a singular state of existence. Another way to address this problem is to energize and enliven the dynamics whereby tension and opposition are resolved and equilibrium is restored. Preachers in this style can work on making even modest resolution into an exciting and wonderful occurrence of God's grace so that it will not be tamed into a manageable, predictable ending to the Christian faith story.

The great strength of this faith story is its ability to communicate narrative closure and fullness without communicating that this closure is contrived or interventionist. The happy ending in this style is not overplayed or dressed up in any way. It gains a realism and clarity that is not achieved when an extraordinary, deus ex machina form of narrative resolution is present.

NEGOTIATING A HEARING

Another strength of this style is that it is the most easily negotiated theosymbolic style of all. It represents a fairly safe middle ground on which compatibilities with other styles are easily found. The low-positive style permits the ample voicing of both tension and opposition; although most tensivists and oppositionalists are suspicious of here-and-now resolution, they are more willing to hear such resolutions as restorations of order or equilibrium than to hear them as fantastic or miraculous interventions that transform the whole nature of reality.

For those who expect some form of powerful and dynamic resolution to the narrative lack in the Christian faith story, the low-positive style is also potentially compatible. Although restored equilibrium may not be enough of a resolution for some, it will suffice if it is energized appropriately as an act of God's grace and goodness. In this case, a hearing for the low-positive style can be negotiated among those who maintain our next style, the high-positive style.

High-Positive Style

This theosymbolic style creates a faith story with a "successful mediation" that not only nullifies the impact of the story's central problem or lack but also establishes a "gain" or "increase" over the initial state of order in the story.[32] In other words, the story culminates not in equilibrium but in a state in which something new or additional has been added. In the high-positive style the disturbances caused by the opponent serve as a foil to set off the communication of the object by the giver. The subject is strongly identified and allied with the helper. The helper has unique, superabundant powers and is not only adequate to nullify the impact of the opponent but also able to exploit the opponent's presence in the narrative structure to great advantage. The giver is powerful and independent and not only is giving the anticipated object to the receiver but also is giving even more than that object to the receiver.

The object is not only what the giver has been attempting to communicate all along but also something exceptional and superlative. The object reflects a structural state of surplus. When surplus is present, the giver can communicate freely not only what is necessary for the receiver but also more and greater things. Typical semantic faces for this object include new life, second birth, the gifts of the Spirit, eternal life, the kingdom of heaven, and abundant life. Again, these are simply diverse meanings that are sometimes given to the narrative structural state of surplus.

The case of David illustrates a high-positive style. David's theosymbolic structure looks like Figure 6. In David's theosymbolic structure the opponent is dramatically overshadowed by the powerful qualities of both giver and helper. Refusal to surrender one's will to God is a significant problem, but it is subordinated and to some extent exploited within the structure to support the clear, extraordinary advantages of the object, spiritual rebirth and eternal life. The helper is very strong. Christ is victorious over sin and death and the Son of God who is Lord of Life and has the power to forgive sins. The church is a powerful extension of Christ, both sharing and defending the gospel in this world. The Bible is also extremely pow-

---

32. See Maranda and Maranda, *Structural Models,* 36; and Crossan, *The Dark Interval,* 52.

FIGURE 6
David's Theosymbolic Structure

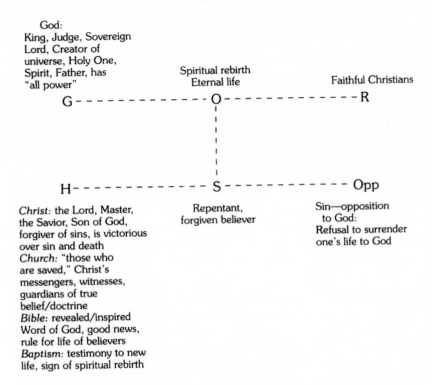

God:
King, Judge, Sovereign
Lord, Creator of
universe, Holy One,
Spirit, Father, has
"all power"

Spiritual rebirth
Eternal life

Faithful Christians

G — — — — — — — — — — — — O — — — — — — — — — — — R

Christ: the Lord, Master,
the Savior, Son of God,
forgiver of sins, is victorious
over sin and death
Church: "those who
are saved," Christ's
messengers, witnesses,
guardians of true
belief/doctrine
Bible: revealed/inspired
Word of God, good news,
rule for life of believers
Baptism: testimony to new
life, sign of spiritual rebirth

Repentant,
forgiven believer

Sin—opposition
to God:
Refusal to surrender
one's life to God

H — — — — — — — — — — — S — — — — — — — — — — — Opp

erful, a revelation from God and the definitive standard for the life
of faith. Baptism is a strong helper in David's preaching. It occurs
frequently as a cipher for spiritual rebirth and a sign of true belief.
The community and individuals are subjects who are totally subordinated to and identified with the helper. Their lives as repentant,
forgiven sinners are functions of the helper's activity on their behalf.
The object that is given in David's theosymbolic structure is not simply the nullification of the impact of the opponent (sin, opposition to
God) and a restored equilibrium; it is a gift far exceeding what this
initial state would suggest: spiritual rebirth and eternal life, a whole
new reality that has no end.

When David preaches a sermon on the Mary and Martha text, he
focuses on the forgiving power of the Savior to which Mary has
surrendered and to which Martha is called. The sermon carries a

mood of surplus: Something incredible is being offered to both women and although they do not yet know what it is, Mary has begun to surrender her life to it. Christ brings spiritual rebirth and eternal life into the home of the women that day, and Mary responds to it, even though doing so meant turning her back on Martha and the serving of dinner. The way Martha misses the mark, whether it is by hiding or not, is only a foil to set off the wonders of what is being offered to the world in Jesus Christ. Instead of communicating simply that "we have overcome that," the sermon communicates that "we have been given more than we ever could have imagined." God is already communicating not simply the restoration of wholeness in our lives but far greater things.

CONSIDERATIONS

The high-positive theosymbolic style in preaching promotes a *permutational* worldview. Tension and opposition, although mildly disruptive, offer opportunities for great gain and increase in the life of the individual or community. The congregation may be cast as a community that is totally committed to or identified with a powerful, active helper and sees itself as an extension of the role of the helper; members perceive expressions of lack as opportunities for tremendous gain in their own lives and in the lives of others. Regardless of the semantic content of this structure, the vision of a permutational object dominates the preacher's picture of the way things really are.

The basic problem with this style is that it can seem sensationalistic or emotionalistic to many. It can be too positive and too prone to excess for its own sake. Everything seems to take place in another world, not in this world. People are asked to step into roles and models of self-perception that have little to do with what they are really thinking or feeling.

Along with this perception of sensationalism comes the perception of manipulation. A kind of herd instinct seems to force people to abandon rationality. Many may be troubled that lack within the faith story is principally a foil or setup for narrative gain. Lack seems to have no reality of its own, except to provide opportunity for the community to celebrate victory over it. This style promotes the feeling that ordinary life is not taken seriously. Ordinary reality is manipulated in favor of a superreality.

The best way to surmount this problem is to be certain that the narrative gain is specific and that it relates to a real, distinct, and uncontrived lack. Preachers in this style should think clearly about the object-opponent relationship and be sure of a real correlation between these two actants in their faith story. Surplus does not mean unrelated, random excess. Even when something extra is given, it should correspond to what has been lacking.

At the same time, preachers will want to unpack the actual dynamics whereby the helper enables the receiver to stand in the pathway of this gain. In other words, preachers will not bypass the articulation of the fullness of the Christian faith story. In this way, preachers will avoid the quick and constant leap to emotional or sensational cliché in order to move the congregation quickly into the semantic field of the glorious object.

The strength of this style is that it takes seriously the tremendous power of the gospel in human life. It recognizes clearly and unapologetically that the gospel can make a tremendous difference in the lives of people. This style also recognizes that the Christian life has much to celebrate. It invites adoration, thanksgiving, and the outpouring of human emotion.

NEGOTIATING A HEARING

In order to negotiate a hearing among equilibrists, the permutationalist must demonstrate the clear adequacy of mediation in the faith story and allow that it is enough, sufficient grace for living. This demonstration must be done first, before celebrating the gain, the final and most significant fact that a new reality is inaugurated in our midst.

The tensivist often reacts to this style as consolationist and as cheap grace. Negotiating a hearing for this model among those who are in a reactionary position or where this model is maintained in a reactionary fashion is extremely difficult. In order to negotiate a hearing among tensivists and oppositionalists, the permutationalist must be careful to take the tensive and oppositional nature of reality seriously. As we have already suggested, the preacher must not exploit tensivity and opposition as mere stepping-stones to the brighter side of the Christian story. Only when the permutationalist seasons his or her "victorious Christianity" with clear acknowledgments

FIGURE 7
Giver-Object Reversal Model

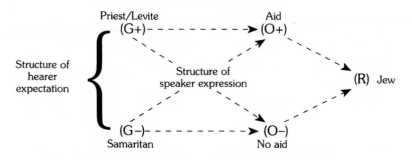

of where the victory comes from and what it addresses will a hearing be negotiated more broadly than among those of like mind.

Reversal Style

The reversal style creates a faith story in which an opposition or problem (lack) is introduced where none previously existed. This style takes what is normally developed into tension, opposition, equilibrium, or permutation and introduces a contradiction that suggests that we have been dealing with the wrong deck of cards all along.[33] According to Crossan, the structure of this faith story resembles the structure of some biblical parables in which the "structure of hearer expectation" is reversed in the "structure of expression" within the parable.[34] For instance, in the parable of the Good Samaritan in Luke 10:25-29 and 10:36, the structure of expectation for Luke's hearers was that the Priest and Levite would be the ones to give aid to the languishing Jew by the roadside. In the structure of speaker expression, however, this expectation is reversed. It is a Samaritan, an enemy, who offers aid.

Crossan notes that narrative reversal tends to occur along the axis of communication (G-O-R) on which the giver gives an object to a

---

33. Crossan calls this a "parabolic" story. Parables, in Crossan's words, are the "polar, or binary, opposite of myth." As long as there is the "creation of contrast" the result is parable. However, "if the storyteller starts to mediate the newly created contrast, the story starts slipping into . . . myth" (*The Dark Interval,* 54–55).
34. Ibid., 66.

FIGURE 8
David's Giver-Object Reversal Structure

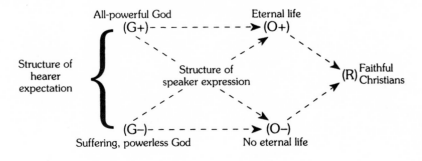

receiver. These actants constitute the basic terms and relations in the narrative. The assumed relationship between these actants is usually reversed in the reversal style.

One model is giver-object reversal. In this model, the receiver remains constant and the giver-object relation is reversed. The result in the parable of the Good Samaritan looks like Figure 7. The crossing arrows on the inside show the reversal of hearer expectation in the structure of the speaker's expression.

The axis of communication in David's faith story looks like this:

All-powerful God	Eternal life	Believers
(G) - - - - - - - - - - ->(O) - - - - - - - - - -> (R)		

A giver-object reversal on this axis in David's homiletical faith story would create a structure that looks like Figure 8. In this theological structure, the preacher is reversing the congregational (hearer) expectation that eternal life is given by God, who is characterized primarily as all-powerful. Instead, the preacher creates contradiction and contrast, showing in sermons that paradoxically a suffering, powerless God is the giver of eternal life and that the all-powerful God is not the God who gives eternal life.

Another option, according to Crossan, is an object-receiver reversal. This reversal establishes the giver instead of the receiver as the stable element, and the reversal is a reversal of expectations regard-

FIGURE 9
Great Banquet Reversal Structure

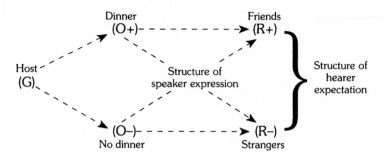

FIGURE 10
David's Object-Receiver Reversal Structure

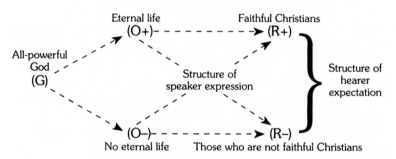

ing the relationship between receiver and object. Crossan uses the story of the Great Banquet, especially as it is told in Luke 14:16-24, as an example.[35] In this story, a host invites friends to dinner. When they refuse he invites strangers, who accept the invitation. The basic structure of the story, then, looks like Figure 9.

Reversing the axis of communication in David's faith story in this way would yield a theological structure like Figure 10. In this model, the all-powerful God can choose to whom the gift of eternal life will be given. The expectation that only faithful Christians will receive

---

35. Ibid., 118. Crossan compares Luke's version of this story to Matthew's and to the version in the Gospel of Thomas. His basic structure is a distillation of his analyis of these various renderings of the story.

FIGURE 11
Mary and Martha Reversal Structure

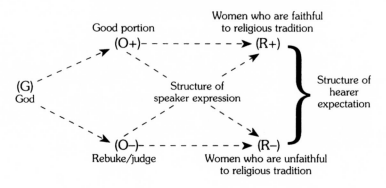

God's gifts is reversed in the expression of the speaker. Again, a new contrast or contradiction is introduced where none previously existed.

In a sermon on the Mary and Martha text, let us assume that the sermon is being preached in a conservative church that has begun to debate whether women should be ordained to the Christian ministry. The reversal structure would look like Figure 11.

The sermon acknowledges that the bulk of Judeo-Christian history and tradition takes it for granted that women are not to be taught or apprenticed by rabbis or church leaders and are not to become either candidates for ministry or ordained ministers and priests. If women are faithful to this tradition, then they will receive God's favor and blessing [(G) → (O+) → (R+)]. Likewise, women who are unfaithful to this tradition will receive God's rebuke and should be rebuked by others, just as Martha desires that Jesus reprimand Mary for her behavior [(G) → (O–) → (R–)]. This result is what the congregation assumes and expects.

In fact, God does just the opposite, as the Mary and Martha story illustrates. First of all, Jesus breaks with religious tradition and teaches a woman. Then, Mary breaks out of her traditional role and sits, as a disciple would, at his feet to listen to his teaching. For this act of unfaithfulness to her tradition, she is honored by Jesus as choosing "the good portion, which shall not be taken away from her"

[(G) → (O+) → (R–)]. Not only this, but Jesus rebukes the woman (Martha) who, in her simple faithfulness to her religious tradition, is not only missing the good portion herself but is trying to stop her sister, Mary, from partaking of it [(G) → (O–) → (R+)]. Not only is Mary honored for being unfaithful to her religious tradition but also Martha is rebuked for being faithful to hers. A new contrast or antithesis is emerging between those who are faithful to God's calling, which makes them unfaithful to their religious tradition, and those who are faithful to their religious tradition but are unfaithful to God's calling (of others and themselves).

When the preacher has a reversal theosymbolic style, the final structural state for the larger homiletical faith story is a state of flux or transition. The fundamental premises of Christian faith, the actants along the axis of communication [(G) → (O) → (R)], are constantly undermined. New relationships are created between established characters in the larger narrative structure so that the entire structure is called constantly into question and reopened for further investigation.

CONSIDERATIONS

The reversal theosymbolic style in preaching promotes an *iconoclastic* worldview. New tensions and oppositions are introduced where none existed before. Old tensions and oppositions are discarded as irrelevant as new tensions and oppositions emerge. Attempts to resolve these new tensions and oppositions are seldom made when this style is maintained intentionally. Not even a low-negative embracing of irresolution is acceptable. To adopt any of the earlier means of dealing with antithesis (low-negative, high-negative, low-positive, high-positive) would be to sacrifice the iconoclastic worldview and begin to move toward the nonmediations, failing mediations, and successful mediations of other styles and worldviews. The iconoclastic worldview requires the constant creation of new unmediated antitheses so that flux and transition are maintained. Congregations are sometimes characterized as those who are committed to a God who cannot be storied, who is elusive, surprising, able to change and to bring about change at any time, giving different kinds of gifts to different kinds of people, and upsetting treasured expectations and agendas. Regardless of the semantic content of the structure, the iconoclastic vision of fundamental premises in permanent transition dominates the picture the preacher paints of the way things really are.

The major problem with this style is that if it is maintained as a dominant style it can communicate that the Christian faith story is completely contradictory to the world of our human senses and reason. The Christian faith is never what we think or feel that it is. It does not stand still. It is always shifting and changing, a kind of chameleon reality that cannot be recognized because the moment it is identified it changes color.

The only way for partially solving this problem is providing some substantial development of the implications of new contrasts or tensions that emerge from the reversal style, which will mean using one of the previous theosymbolic styles to start the congregation down the narrative pathway suggested by a new contrast. The low-negative style, for instance, with its refusal of mediations or resolutions, would at least provide the preacher the opportunity to establish a new axis of communication as one that reveals at least something about the order of reality in which we live.

For example, once the congregation has begun to see that the powerless, suffering God is the giver of eternal life, a whole set of new assumptions comes with this perception. A new axis of communication lends itself to new conceptualizations of the opponent, subject, and helper. A new positive axis of communication would look like this:

Powerless suffering God   Eternal life   Faithful people of God
$$(G) - - - - - - - - - - - \rightarrow (O) - - - - - - - - - - - \rightarrow (R)$$

To this axis might be added other actants and axes that introduce the possibility of a new, full-scale narrative structure in one of the previous modes. For instance, the other actants could look like this:

$$(H) - - - - - - - - - - - \rightarrow (S) - - - - - - - - - \rightarrow (Opp)$$
Crucified Lord   Obedient disciples   Principalities and powers

New tensions, new opponents, and new insights about the nature of the subject, object, and helper can be explored by the preacher. In order to remain true to the reversal style, however, the preacher will, at some point, reverse even these new insights.

Another problem with this style is that it can indicate an inability or unwillingness to assume the theological responsibility on the part of the preacher to commit to a program of thought and action. The preacher becomes a kind of "permanent revolutionary"[36] who is preoccupied with subverting the status quo.[37] He or she is in a permanent state of theological contradiction with the congregation on just about everything.

For this reason, the reversal style is best used temporarily and for constructive purposes. The preacher needs to examine his or her motives for maintaining this style to determine whether it is being used on behalf of the congregation and their needs and concerns or whether it is simply a manifestation of an inability or unwillingness to belong, participate, and assume authority.

The strength of this style is its ability to keep congregations mindful of the limited and fragile nature of all theological worldviews. This style shows us the seams and edges of the faith stories we shape in order that they might not be absolutized or become rigid.[38] This style reminds us that language and all symbolic means of adding shape and form to God's life and activity in our midst are limited and inadequate. It reminds us, in the words of T. S. Eliot, that "human kind cannot bear very much reality,"[39] and that we often impose narrative shape and epistemological order upon a reality that is largely shapeless and unknowable. It is a style that, when properly used, can be humbling and in some cases revelatory, reopening worldviews so that they might include more reality.

NEGOTIATING A HEARING

The reversal stylist can negotiate a hearing only by taking seriously the assumed relations that are being reversed and allowing for

36. Erich Neumann writes about the "permanent revolutionary" in his explication of ancient hero myths in which the focus of the heroic quest is on "the slaying of the father." The permanent revolutionary is the hero who refuses "to become a father and assume power." This refusal "seems to him a guarantee of perpetual youth." He is the rugged individualist who is "not prepared to 'be his age' and accept his limitations" (*The Origins and History of Consciousness* [Princeton: Princeton University Press, 1973], 190).

37. In the words of Crossan, the "world" established by the previous narrative structures is "subverted" by this reversal structure, and the possibility of change is introduced (*The Dark Interval*, 59–60).

38. Ibid., 56.

39. T. S. Eliot, *Four Quartets* (New York: Harcourt, Brace & World, 1971), 14.

at least some positive truth in those relations. Otherwise, the reversalist will be perceived as an insincere trickster. Jesus took seriously the expectation that the priest and Levite would help the man lying by the roadside. This expectation is not simply a straw assumption he needs in order to work his reversal; it is a real assumed relation that he acknowledges time and again to be an expectation that is not only legitimate but also even redemptive in its true conception.

Likewise, in preaching the Mary and Martha text to a conservative church, the preacher needs to take seriously the expected relationship between the "good portion" and women who are faithful to their religious tradition. This assumption is not to be treated lightly or maliciously, as if no truth were anywhere near this idea. When this happens, the reversal style degenerates into a subtle form of invective, and no negotiation is possible. For the reversal style to work, then, the preacher must come back again and again and give serious attention to the assumed relations that are being reversed in his or her preaching. The congregation must be given the sense that the assumed relations they hold so dear are capable of much truth and insight but are also blinding them to a more important truth or insight that can be seen only when these assumptions are reversed.

APPLYING THEOSYMBOLIC CODE

We have now had an opportunity to explore the theosymbolic code and the five principal ways this code sponsors the theological worldview of congregations today. The third layer of our rhetorical schema looks like this:

Theosymbolic Code

Content: Christian symbols as they are ordered in the preacher's theological structure or faith story.

Intertext: Worldview: the congregation's picture of the way things are or their image of the order of the world. It includes ethos, the underlying attitude the community has toward themselves and the world.

Styles: Code styles sponsor intertext styles (Table 7).

TABLE 7
Theosymbolic Code and Intertext Styles

Code Style	Sponsors	Intertext Style
Negative		*Worldview of lack*
1. Low		1. Tensive worldview
2. High		2. Oppositional worldview
Positive		*Worldview of plenitude*
1. Low		1. Equilibrational worldview
2. High		2. Permutational worldview
Reversal		*Iconoclastic worldview*

In this chapter I have suggested that preaching sponsors in five different styles the theological worldview of congregations. Let me again indicate a broader analytic process through which the preacher can put this information into intentional, strategic use.

Homiletical Analysis

Begin with an analysis of the content and style of the theosymbolic code in your preaching. Use the process and questions suggested earlier to analyze your theosymbolic content and style. (Look again at the concluding chapter for an example of sermon decoding.) Again, if you do not use a manuscript, tape your sermons for a few months and transcribe them so that they can be studied more easily.

Congregational Analysis

The analysis of congregational worldview is not a simple matter. James Hopewell's process in *Congregation: Stories and Structures* may be helpful. His empiric, canonic, gnostic, and charismatic worldviews have significant correlations with the tensive, oppositional, equilibrational, and permutational worldviews we have examined. Hopewell's focus on particular semantic content as definitive of worldviews rather than on structural relationships between actants and their relative structural strength, however, may complicate your task and keep you from seeing where significant correlations or differences lie.

Another way to approach this task would be to take the idea inventory of your sermon planning groups (from chapter 2) and do the same kind of short analysis on them that you can do with your own idea inventory. Place the narrative structure on top of the congregation's seven plus or minus two basic ideas and look for the basic theological worldview indicated by this narrative structure.

You might also conduct a congregational interview process in which a cross-section of your congregation is invited to tell their faith story. You could then conduct an actantial analysis of their individual stories and look for a dominant model based on the five models outlined previously.

Theological and Pastoral Analysis

Analyze theologically and pastorally what you are doing and what you need to do.

Theological Reflection

Reflect on your theosymbolic style and the theological worldview you are sponsoring in your preaching. Do they reflect your personal commitments? Do some actants in your faith story need more intentional development or more frequent appearances in your preaching in order for your homiletical faith story to reflect more clearly your actual faith commitments? Do some relationships between actants need attention for your homiletical faith story to be true to your faith commitments? What theological traditions or paradigms are you drawing from to tell this homiletical faith story? What further reading can you do to strengthen this faith story?

Pastoral Reflection

Look for similarities and differences between your homiletical faith story and the dominant faith story of your congregation. If possible, discuss your findings with members of the congregation so that your decisions and commitments will be shared.

Ask a number of questions that will enable you to think through the pastoral dimensions of your findings. Do significant points of conflict or confrontation exist between your homiletical faith story and your congregation's fundamental faith story? Are the relationships between actants the same, only with different semantic content? (In other words, are you promoting a similar worldview with different theological content?) Is your theosymbolic style and worldview entirely different or alien to your congregation's? How different? Are they open to the style and worldview you represent? Are you open to the style and worldview they represent? What compatibilities exist between the content and style of your theosymbolic code and the content and style of the congregation's theosymbolic code?

Conscious Commitment

The final step in your process is to commit yourself to an intentional encoding of a faith story in your preaching. Focus your continuing education and theological reading around the theosymbolic style and worldview to which you are committed. Be sure that the faith story you tell is one that you can own enthusiastically and that will be meaningful and helpful for your congregation.

If this larger process is too much for you to try at this time, reflect on your current theosymbolic style and worldview. Consider ways to strengthen this style and negotiate a better hearing for it. Ask yourself if it is true to your faith commitments and to the needs of your congregation. Above all else, as you prepare sermons, try to become conscious and strategic in the way that you encode the Christian faith story in your preaching.

4

THE CULTURAL CODE

Culture is a telescopic concept. Many subcultures exist within the larger culture of Western, American society. We speak of the subcultures of the South, the North, the beach, or the office and of the subcultures of the family, the business world, the seminary, or our church. Each of these subcultures is like a language the individual learns in order to generate or express certain experiences.

CONTENT

The content of the cultural code is every reference within a sermon to the broader culture in which the congregation lives its daily life. The word *culture* is not an easy word to define, especially as the discipline of anthropology has claimed culture as its central analytical datum. Stated simply, a *culture* is "the content of socialization."[1] It is that entire body of received information: ideas, opinions, attitudes, values, beliefs, and experiences that constitute a particular social and historical moment or epoch and are appropriated by an individual and community as the common life of humanity within prescribed boundaries.

A preacher can in no way gain access to uncultured experience. Whether culture is viewed as fundamentally generative of experience

---

1. David Filbeck, *Social Context and Proclamation: A Socio-Cognitive Study in Proclaiming the Gospel Cross-Culturally* (Pasadena, Calif.: William Carey Library, 1985), 49.

or as fundamentally expressive of experience,[2] the fact remains that both culture and experience are caught up together and are not easily separated, especially at the macro level of human experience with which most of preaching deals. Whenever a preacher wishes to refer a sermon to the experience of the congregation, therefore, he or she must refer to the culture within which that experience finds expression. Therefore, we will speak of a cultural code that sponsors an intertext of experience. Each way of encoding culture sponsors a particular way of textualizing experience and of shaping experience in language.

The cultural code in preaching typically manifests itself in many different kinds of content: illustrations of all types (analogies, examples, metaphors), clichés, appeals to authority, maxims, proverbs, common opinions, assumptions regarding manners, morals, appearance, furniture, furnishings, clothing, design, references to the arts, literature, public and private ceremonies, sports, politics, customs, habits of eating and body care, modes of livelihood, social organization, and so on. From a rhetorical perspective, these cultural references serve a dual function. They legitimate the sermon by rooting it in a particular culture, and they legitimate a particular culture. A content analysis of the cultural code of your preaching for the past year or so will provide you with a clear picture of what the legitimate and legitimating culture for your preaching tends to be.

The best way to accomplish this analysis is to go back through your past year's preaching and do a culture inventory. Jot down on paper all the subcultures to which you refer in each sermon, the cultural reference points for all appeals, assumptions, and illustrations. Then group these subcultures into categories until you have determined the basic subcultures that inform your preaching. Although this list is far from exhaustive, here are some fairly typical subcultures that find their way into American preaching:

---

2. The chicken-egg debate regarding the relationship between experience and culture is probably unresolvable. For those whom George Lindbeck calls "experiential-expressivists," culture is derivative from experience. He lumps together in this category theologians such as Mircea Eliade, Paul Tillich, and Alfred North Whitehead. Lindbeck, in contrast, advocates a "cultural-linguistic" approach that reverses this relationship and claims that inner experiences must be viewed as derivative from cultural-linguistic foundations (*The Nature of Doctrine: Religion and Theology in a Post-Liberal Age* [Philadelphia: Westminster Press, 1984], 34–35).

The family	Popular wisdom	Fashion
Academia	Sports	Government
Seminary	The military	Politics
The church	Television	The early church
The neighborhood	Patriotism	Movies
Advertising	Popular psychology	Popular music
Literature	Business management	Drama
Science	Law	The pastoral ministry

Then examine how each subculture is conceived in your preaching. Ask three basic questions of each of your primary subcultures. First of all, is each subculture given a negative or positive profile in your preaching? Some subcultures are okay and some are not okay. Some are "us," and some are "them." Some subcultures are split down the middle, based on the stereotyping of positive and negative aspects. For instance, some preachers see a positive culture of the family (perhaps with no history of divorce, wife at home, husband at work, children obedient) and a negative culture of the family (perhaps with single parent, working mother, children in a day-care center and "displaying behavior problems").

Second, is each subculture stereotypical or open and inclusive of variety? In other words, is each subculture a multifaceted, dynamic culture in a state of constant change and renewal, or is it a predictable, stationary culture, always displaying the same characteristics? For instance, the culture of the family can include a wide variety of models and faces—nuclear family, single-parent family, family in therapy, family at home, family fighting, family loving—or the culture of the family can always be used in the same, predictable way, that of family equals nuclear family.

Third, as you review your responses to the first two questions, how is your encoding of each subculture expressive of political, socioeconomic, class, gender, or racial-ethnic assumptions? This question is designed to help you determine the contours of the cultural ideology you are communicating through your cultural code. A determination of your positive and negative subcultures and of cultural stereotypes is the first step toward the determination of the implicit ideology carried by the cultural code of your preaching. For instance, a positive stereotyping of a nuclear family with at-home mother and obedient children, coupled with a negative stereotyping of a single-parent family with working mother and delinquent children, supports a conservative, upper-middle-class, white, authoritarian, nonfeminist ideology.

I have written elsewhere about the communicative power of the cultural code in preaching.[3] The cultural code is a subtle or not-so-subtle transmitter of stereotypes, prejudices, and ideology in preaching. Often this code counteracts the kinds of messages communicated at the level of the semantic code in preaching. For instance, the preacher whose semantic code is replete with ideas about the equalitarian, just, and forgiving life of the Christian community and whose cultural references are mainly to the authoritarian, backbiting, eye-for-an-eye culture of Wall Street business will introduce a certain amount of code dissonance between the cultural and semantic codes in preaching. Different and contradictory messages are being sent at each level of coding. For those who decode sermons via their culture and experience rather than via their systems of meaning and truth, this contradiction may become problematic, even insurmountable.

When I speak about the *contents* of the cultural code throughout the remainder of this chapter, I will substitute the term *homiletical culture*, which will indicate the total culture, including all subcultures, to which a preacher refers in his or her preaching.

Because much of cultural coding is done unconsciously in preaching, a periodic content analysis of this code in your preaching is very important to be certain that your homiletical culture is not in a direct or subtle confrontation with the content of your semantic code. This content analysis is also important because it is the first step in determining the style of cultural encoding you tend to emphasize and the way that it affects the intertext of experience in your congregation.

INTERTEXT OF EXPERIENCE

The cultural code sponsors an intertext of experience, a homiletical shaping of experience in language. According to Bernard Meland, experience is "an internal ordering of responses [to events] in individual lives." This ordering of responses is "channeled" inwardly in

3. "The Other Side of Sermon Illustration," *Journal for Preachers* 12 (1989): 2–4.

"individual memories, sensibilities, and bodily characteristics which make up any individual psyche" and channeled outwardly into a corporate "structure of experience" or "culture."[4] Culture, then, is a kind of outward sedimentation of experience, a "structure of experience" that mirrors (imperfectly) a particular way in which a group of people order their responses to the eventfulness of life. A culture reproduces that ordering of responses (experience) and is capable of generating further experiences that follow from that same ordering. The preacher's cultural code, therefore, sponsors a way of experiencing the Christian faith and of internally ordering our responses to the Christ event.

Again, the biblical text constrains and authorizes the preacher's cultural code and textualization of experience. As Hans Frei, George Lindbeck, and others have noted, the Christian community is, in many respects, "intratextual," a sectarian culture whose experience is defined by the boundaries of the biblical text.[5] For many preachers the experience of the Christ event is an experience of learning and living the cultural grammar of the Bible.[6] Other preachers will feel compelled, however, "to expand the borders of the Christian imagination, finding Christ's presence in previously unknown places,"[7] and

4. Bernard Meland, *The Realities of Faith* (New York: Oxford University Press, 1962), 210.

5. George A. Lindbeck, "The Sectarian Future of the Church," in *The God Experience: Essays in Hope*, ed. Joseph P. Whelan, S.J. (New York: Newman Press, 1971), 226; and *The Nature of Doctrine*; Hans Frei, *The Eclipse of Biblical Narrative: A Study in Eighteenth and Nineteenth Century Hermeneutics* (New Haven: Yale University Press, 1974); Stanley Hauerwas, *Truthfulness and Tragedy: Further Investigations into Christian Ethics* (Notre Dame, Ind.: University of Notre Dame Press, 1977); Jacob Neusner and Ernst Frerichs, eds., *"To See Ourselves as Others See Us": Christians, Jews, "Others" in Late Antiquity* (Chico, Calif.: Scholars Press, 1985); and Brian Stock, *The Implications of Literacy: Written Language and Models of Interpretation in the Eleventh and Twelfth Centuries* (Princeton: Princeton University Press, 1983).

6. Lindbeck, *The Nature of Doctrine*, 119.

7. Gary L. Comstock, "Two Types of Narrative Theology," *Journal of the American Academy of Religion* 55 (Spring 1987): 707. Examples of this perspective on the biblical text and Christian culture and experience include David Tracy, *The Analogical Imagination: Christian Theology and the Culture of Pluralism* (New York: Crossroad, 1981); Paul Ricoeur, *The Conflict of Interpretations: Essays in Hermeneutics* (Evanston, Ill.: Northwestern University Press, 1974); and "The Specificity of Religious Language," in *Biblical Hermeneutics, Semeia* 4 (1975): 107; Julian Hartt, *Theological Method Imagination* (New York: Seabury Press, 1977); and "Theological Investments in Story: Some Comments on Recent Developments and Some Proposals," *Journal of the American Academy of Religion* 52 (1984): 117.

search for the cultural grammar of the Bible beyond the boundaries of the Christian community. This group of preachers will not be able to deny the cultural and experiential interiority of the community of the Bible. They will simply aspire, after the pattern of the apostle Paul, "to make the Gospel speak to the Greeks, the Kantians, and the utilitarians"[8] and to expand the experience of the Christian faith to include those whose religious experience is not yet bounded by the biblically rooted culture of the Christian church.

STYLES

As we have indicated, the cultural code in preaching sponsors (vouches for, promotes, and responds to) an intertext of experience in the church. Let us now investigate further how sponsorship is accomplished and the variety of styles it takes in contemporary preaching.

Vouching for the Intertext

The intertext of experience is vouched for most strongly when preachers consciously and intentionally refer the contents of the semantic code, the sermon's meaning (whether an insight, hypothesis, assertion, or argument), to a homiletical culture capable of mediating the experiential core of this meaning. The preacher, therefore, must be consciously committed to some form of continuity or relationship between the meaning of the gospel and culture and encode it in sermons if sermons are to vouch for a particular form of experience that includes within it the experience of the Christian faith.

For instance, I can leave the assertion that "Jesus Christ empowers the marginalized to come out of hiding" as an abstract concept—a provocative idea, certainly, but only vaguely related to human experience. My congregation can freely associate about the cultural and experiential correlates of this assertion—hide-and-go-seek, hiding from the law, hiding from the obnoxious kid at school, political empowerment, flower power, power hitter, and so on. When this much cultural latitude and experiential speculation is consistently

8. Comstock, "Two Types of Narrative Theology," 707.

permitted in preaching, the cultural code becomes weak. The congregation is left wondering how this or any assertion is related to their own experience. They may wonder if any experiential coordinate for the meaning of the gospel exists in my preaching at all. They are left without any guidance about how to relate homiletical meaning to the structure of experience or culture that they as a congregation inhabit.

By contrast, I can seek out a subculture that is capable of mediating the experiential core of the assertion that "Jesus Christ empowers the marginalized to come out of hiding." What might this subculture be? I may look to the biblical text to provide some clues. What about the subculture of the home? After all, this event took place in the home of Mary and Martha. Perhaps I should include an illustration that shows how the home can become a hiding place for some women, a culturally sanctioned and ritualized way of turning from themselves. Maybe here the gospel of Christ's empowerment can make a difference. Many vignettes from the novels of Doris Lessing or Margaret Atwood, for example, could be used to illustrate this.[9] What about uniting the subcultures of theological education (Jesus was a rabbi and Mary a student), the family (Martha was Mary's sister), and the religious community (both women were Jews)? Maybe I should tell the story of a woman I knew during my student days at seminary who received weekly phone calls from her mother and members of a prayer group at her former church who hoped she would soon "come to her senses" and abandon seminary education. Because of this reaction, she felt unable to go back to her home church, the community in which her faith had been nurtured. Perhaps the empowerment of Jesus Christ could make a difference in this circumstance.

When I introduce the cultural code in this way or in any other way, I am vouching for a certain experience and a particular form of experience. I am locating that experience somewhere, showing where and when it occurs. I am saying, in essence, "the experience of hiding and empowerment exists at home," and "the experience of hiding and empowerment exists at the juncture of theological education, the

9. Doris Lessing, *Martha Quest* (London: Panther Books, 1972); and *A Proper Marriage* (London: Panther Books, 1972); and Margaret Atwood, *The Edible Woman* (Toronto: McClelland and Steward, 1969).

family, and the religious community." The minute I encode such cultural data, I am not only drawing forth a dynamic equivalent to the biblical text but also vouching for a particular experience of the meaning of the gospel.

Promoting the Intertext

There are four fundamental styles of encoding culture in preaching. Each style directly or indirectly promotes a similar intertext of experience in the community. These styles are defined according to the kind of relationship the preacher establishes between the semantic code and the cultural code and between homiletical meaning and homiletical culture. I have adapted these styles from H. Richard Niebuhr's classic work, *Christ and Culture*.[10] These styles are (1) identification, (2) dialectical, (3) dualist, and (4) sectarian.

Identification Style

In this style, the preacher identifies homiletical meaning with the obvious features of his or her homiletical culture and places no qualifiers on the use of cultural information. This style shows little or no theological critique of the homiletical culture and no effort to be selective either of what is used within that culture or of the depth of the cultural information. The sermon's meaning becomes culturally idiomatic. It is so identified with a particular homiletical culture as to be inseparable from it in any way. In other words, the preacher's semantic code and cultural code merge and become nearly identical. To hear a preacher's homiletical culture is to hear the meaning of the sermon and vice versa.

Media preachers often make use of this style because it accentuates the common ground that exists between the gospel and culture. A good example of this kind of preaching is that of Robert Schuller. Schuller permits a complete identification of the gospel with an older American utilitarian subculture of self-help and a newer pop-

---

10. H. Richard Niebuhr, *Christ and Culture* (New York: Harper & Row, 1951). See also William J. Carl III, *Preaching Christian Doctrine* (Philadelphia: Fortress Press, 1984), 126–37, for a similar homiletical approach to Niebuhr's categories.

psychological subculture of self-esteem.[11] Another very different example is the preaching of Jerry Falwell, in which the gospel is identified closely with a traditionalist subculture of early American moral and family life and the political subculture of the New Right.[12] Whenever a particular cultural form is so constant and pervasive as to be identified with the meaning of the gospel, the identification style can be said to dominate a preacher's cultural coding.

Let us imagine a sermon on Mary and Martha by a preacher who, like Robert Schuller, identifies the meaning of the gospel with the culture of self-esteem. In this sermon, Martha is hiding from success in life and Mary is successful because she is a "possibility thinker." Although this excerpt is not taken from a sermon but from one of Robert Schuller's books, the congregation might hear this kind of rhetoric:

> Are you disappointed, discouraged and discontented with your level of success? Are you secretly dissatisfied with your present status? Do you want to become a better and more beautiful person than you are today? Would you like to be able to really learn how to be proud of yourself and still not lose genuine humility? Then start dreaming! It's possible! You can become the person you've always wanted to be!
>
> How? There is a KEY—there is a SECRET—there is a WAY—to turn impossible dreams into fantastic accomplishments. I call it *Possibility Thinking*.[13]

The meaning of the sermon is identified with images of success and self-esteem, being a more beautiful person, being proud of yourself, having dreams come true, and achieving fantastic accomplishments.

11. See especially Dennis Voskuil, *Mountains into Goldmines: Robert Schuller and the Gospel of Success* (Grand Rapids: Wm. B. Eerdmans, 1983). Voskuil traces the cultural identification of Schuller's message to popular psychologies of self-actualization and self-fulfillment and, in particular, to Schuller's own brand of self-esteem psychology as set forth in Schuller's book *Self-Esteem: The New Reformation* (Waco, Tex: Word, 1982). He then traces the deeper and older cultural taproots of Schuller's gospel to the "New Thought" tradition of preachers who have wedded the American Dream to "a utilitarian message of self-help through some form of mind-conditioning" (p. 115). Others in this tradition include Phineas Parkhurst Quimby, Mary Baker Eddy, Charles and Myrtle Fillmore, Ralph Waldo Trine, and Norman Vincent Peale.

12. See Gabriel Fackre, *The New Right and Christian Faith* (Grand Rapids: Wm. B. Eerdmans, 1982), 7.

13. Robert Schuller, *You Can Become the Person You Want to Be* (Old Tappan, N.J.: Spire Books, 1973), 12.

The sermon makes no critical distinction between the meaning of the sermon and the cultures of success and self-esteem.

CONSIDERATIONS

The identification style in preaching sponsors an intertext of *ideal* experience in the church. It is ideal because to achieve that form of experience is to appropriate the very meaning of the gospel in its fullness. The congregation is invited to achieve an ideal ordering of responses to (experience of) the Christ event.

This style of preaching tends to relate current experience to an idealized form of experience drawn from either the past or the future. In its conservative forms, experience from the past is idealized, such as the experience of "the traditional family" in Falwell's preaching or "the American dream" in Schuller's preaching. In its liberal forms, ideal experience is projected onto the future, such as the experience of equal rights or "the brotherhood of man."[14] Much of the Jesus Movement[15] preaching of the late sixties and early seventies and some of the utopian preaching of past and present Social Gospel preachers promotes a future vision of ideal experience rooted in a cultural idiom of evolution, progress, and social optimism.[16]

Idealized experience involves ongoing self-judgment. People must constantly assess their relationship to the ideal and ask whether they are achieving it. Experience is ordered in such a way as to reach closer approximations of the ideal.

---

14. H. Richard Niebuhr observes the close relationship between the "Christ against Culture" type of faith and the "Christ of Culture" type. In speaking of the "Christ of Culture" type, Niebuhr notes how closely related the nineteenth-century liberal vision of "the kingdom of God" and the Social Gospel vision of the "brotherhood of man" were to the Jeffersonian cultural hope for a humanity "gathered into one family 'under the bonds of charity, peace, common wants and common aids.'" For many nineteenth-century liberals, the gospel was completely identified with these cultural ideals. Niebuhr noted how fundamentalists often identify Christ with an "older culture," with older "cosmological and biological assumptions . . . about the manner of creation and the earth's destruction," and identify "obedience to Jesus Christ with . . . the maintenance of early American social organization" *(Christ and Culture,* 99–102).

15. See Ronald Enroth, Edward E. Ericson, and C. Breckinridge Peters, *The Jesus People* (Grand Rapids: Wm. B. Eerdmans, 1972).

16. For a look at the cultural roots and influence of Social Gospel preaching in one denomination, see John McClure, "Changes in the Authority, Method and Message of Presbyterian Preaching (UPCUSA) in the Twentieth Century," in *The Confessional Mosaic: Presbyterians and Twentieth Century Theology,* ed. Milton J Coalter, John M. Mulder, and Louis B. Weeks, (Louisville: Westminster/John Knox Press, 1990), 100–101.

One problem with the identification style is that it can become dated and parochial. Cultural idioms change, sometimes very quickly, and congregations are left clinging to archaic cultural and experiential reference points. A friend recently told me of visiting a small chapel near the beach in southern California. The chapel was the home of a small remnant hippie congregation of "ex–Jesus freaks" whose preacher had maintained the countercultural rap session idiom for preaching, despite the fact that he and most of the members of the congregation were now driving Volvos and BMWs. This church has parallels to the church that clings to the archaic cultural idiom of the Westminster divines, King James, and Puritan America in a world of nuclear weapons and acid rain. When cultural idioms rigidify and are closely identified with the meaning of the gospel, preaching can quickly become irrelevant and culturally disconnected.

Another problem with the identification style is the difficulty of assessing and upgrading the quality of the homiletical culture. Quality is especially important in the identification style of preaching because of the tremendously powerful role that the preacher's homiletical culture plays in communicating the gospel. The identificationist sometimes places great value on remaining current in his or her homiletical culture and closely adhering to cultural trends, whether secular or Christian, while failing to assess the quality of the homiletical culture being used. Frequently identificationist preachers *update* their homiletical culture without *upgrading* it. I may update my identification of Martha with the cultural idiom of Eugenia Price's *God Speaks to Women* to the cultural idiom of Maribelle Morgan's *Total Woman*, but what have I gained?

This point brings us to another important observation about the identification style. Because of the importance attributed to a particular homiletical culture in the identification style, that culture, no matter how inadequate or deficient, quickly achieves a superior and final status. This style of preaching often leads to the tacit assumption that the preacher's homiletical culture is the *only* culture for the meaning of the gospel. For Schuller, the culture of self-esteem and success begins as one significant homiletical culture and ends up as the only homiletical culture for the gospel. This identification is perhaps tolerable if this exclusive culture is truly a profound and universal expression of the experience of the gospel,[17] but it is less than tolerable if this culture is simply the most convenient and acceptable for communicating the gospel in a particular geographic locale and socioeconomic environment.

The identification style becomes theologically questionable when the homiletical meaning of the gospel is limited to human ideals. Instead of some things in a culture exemplifying the meaning of the gospel, the gospel begins to stand for certain cultural and experiential standards and ideals. As H. Richard Niebuhr points out, Christ is accommodated to culture, to the best we can be. This adaptation may represent a serious reduction of the power and offense of the gospel.[18]

The strength of the identification style is that it directly affirms everyday, common culture and experience as arenas for God's activity. God is at work in the career track, the traditional American family, and so on. The identification style communicates a profound awareness of the presence and activity of Jesus Christ at the very heart of the culture in which we live.

This style also has tremendous evangelistic potential. Like Paul in his Mars Hill sermon, the preacher accentuates the common ground between the meaning of the gospel and the culture in order to gain a hearing from people whose lives are caught up in an entirely different cultural frame of reference than that of Jesus and his disciples. The offense of the gospel message is played down to earn a hearing from those beyond the walls of the Christian community. The losses are clear when the meaning of the gospel in preaching is identified with a particular homiletical culture. If the preacher is conscious of this identification, however, and makes up for it in other dimensions

17. Schuller attempted to make a case that this was so in his book *Self-Esteem: The New Reformation.*

18. Niebuhr is deeply concerned with preaching and speaks of how "the point of contact they [Christ of culture types] seek to find with their hearers dominates the whole sermon; and in many instances the resultant portrait of Christ is little more than a personification of an abstraction. Jesus stands for the idea of spiritual knowledge; or of logical reason; or of the sense for the infinite; or of the moral law within; or of brotherly love" (*Christ and Culture,* 109).

of church life, the potential at least to be heard by the wider community is greatly increased when this style is used.[19]

NEGOTIATING A HEARING

To paraphrase Schleiermacher, the identification style will appeal to the "enculturated among the despisers of religion,"[20] that is, to those who know little distance or alienation from their culture and who want to have that culture provided with some sense of religious rootedness.[21] It will also appeal to those who yearn for a best culture and an ideal experience. These persons are often not satisfied with the present situation and are either nostalgic for a bygone era or eager for a future one. For these people, the identification of the gospel with a friendly or idealized homiletical culture appeals to a basic need to have values they have already adopted religiously confirmed.

To those hearers who are wary of any identification of the gospel with a particular cultural matrix, who feel themselves alienated from the broader culture in many ways, or who distrust ideals, nostalgia, and futurism, this style of preaching will present a problem. Before identifying Christ with a particular cultural matrix, therefore, the preacher will need to listen carefully to the congregation and discover a homiletical culture that obtains as much congregational agreement as possible and comparably little alienation. Schuller's southern Californian choice of a homiletical culture of self-esteem and success may not work well if your church is located in a small mining village in eastern Kentucky. You will need to work more on a micro than macro level, looking into your neighborhood, its families, patterns of life, and needs, as Schuller did, in order to find effective points of identification. The key to negotiating this style, no matter what identification is made, is to study the immediate culture in which

19. Robert Schuller, for instance, is conscious in his identification of the gospel with popular culture in his worship services at the Crystal Cathedral. He insists that the education program of the church more than makes up for what is lost in this approach.

20. Friedrich Schleiermacher, *On Religion: Speeches to Its Cultured Despisers*, trans. John Oman (New York: Harper & Row, 1958).

21. On the relationship between culture and religion as a quest for rootedness, see Eric O. Springsted, "The Religious Basis of Culture: T. S. Eliot and Simone Weil," *Religious Studies* 25 (March 1989): 105–16.

you are located and decide on an identification with a cultural matrix that is common to your hearers and elicits the least possible alienation.

Although this style is not popular among seminary-trained, parish-based preachers, it can be tremendously successful in situations where church growth is an important priority. A preacher may wish to use this style only temporarily or only in certain circumstances. In any case, this style should always be used with great care and integrated into a larger communication program that includes more critical and prophetic approaches to culture.

Dialectical Style

In the dialectical style, the preacher refuses a wholesale identification of the sermon's meaning with his or her homiletical culture. The preacher is generally suspicious of the adequacy of culture to contain or express the fullness of the gospel and worries about the need to distinguish culture from the gospel, while at the same time expresses some positive relationship between the two. The dialectician will incorporate a *negative* move in his or her cultural coding, to distance homiletical meaning from culture, and a positive move of relating homiletical meaning and culture at selected points. Two dialectical substyles contribute to the accomplishment of this goal: synthetic style and conversion style.[22] Each of these styles relates the meaning of the gospel in the sermon (semantic code) and preacher's homiletical culture (cultural code) without permitting them to be identified with each other.

Synthetic Style

In this style, the preacher carefully seeks levels or aspects of his or her homiletical culture that reflect, in the preacher's estimation, the true nature of things, and coordinates within that culture that reflect

---

22. These styles closely parallel Niebuhr's "synthesist" and "conversionist" types of Christian faith. Niebuhr includes his "dualist" type with these two because of their common interest in preserving the God-givenness of culture without accommodating Christ to that culture. I have moved the dualists into a closer relationship with the "Christ against Culture" type because they tend to have rhetorical similarities and sponsor similar textualizations of Christian experience, despite significant differences on the nature of culture.

God's created order and are thus "previsions,"[23] "figures,"[24] or types of the homiletical meaning being communicated. Only certain things are true to God's creation and deserve to be synthesized (put together, combined) with the meaning of the gospel in the sermon. Therefore, the preacher's cultural code must be critiqued and searched out for its appropriate meaning coordinates. This critique or search constitutes a negative dialectical move—a distancing of the meaning of the gospel to be preached from culture in its totality, a qualification, and a curbing of the preacher's homiletical culture. This preached meaning is then positively synthesized with the preacher's homiletical culture at points where that culture seems to be a true figure or type of some aspect of that meaning.

Carefully selected illustrations—analogies, examples, and metaphors—drawn from a variety of subcultures are fundamental to this style. These do not have to be qualified in any way. Once the preacher has found a figure for the preached meaning in a subcultural matrix, it *is* that meaning. The preacher has no reservation in claiming it as such with boldness. Illustrations do not have to have a central character who is a Christian or a clear representative of Christ and the gospel. The preacher in this style can look deeply into the fabric of ordinary human experience and see figures for the various aspects of the Christian message where Christians are not explicitly involved. These illustrations do not need to have a "moral," a kernel of meaning that is interpreted as a lesser example of "the real (gospel) thing."

This style of preaching has less surface culture. Clichés, common opinions, maxims, and proverbs will be infrequent. Appeals to authority will be more subtle, issuing less from statistics, the media, and common opinions and more from history, philosophy, and the arts.

Although the meaning of the sermon and the preacher's homiletical culture have a very positive relationship in the synthetic style, the preacher's homiletical culture is not identified wholesale with the

---

23. Niebuhr, *Christ and Culture,* 127.

24. Christine Downing, "Typology and the Literary Christ-figure: A Critique," *Journal of the American Academy of Religion* 36 (March 1968): 13. According to Downing, a figure, unlike an archetype, establishes a "formal correspondence between . . . two historical realities rather than between a historical fact and an archetype" (p. 15). A figure is "something real which announces something else, separate in time from it, but also taking place within concrete history" (p. 14).

meaning of the sermon. The meaning that is being preached remains something more than that culture.[25] Culture takes on a sacramental presence in preaching.[26] Through the sacramental (discerning, blessing) actions of the preacher, the something more of the preached gospel meaning is discovered in the something less of his or her homiletical culture. The semantic code and the cultural code are not identical; rather, they share certain coordinates that are the meaning of the gospel in the sermon. They relate as a view does to a mountaintop. The mountaintop is part of the view. Indeed, you could not have the view without the mountaintop. However, the mountaintop is not identical to the view—the full meaning of the gospel—which remains something more.

Edmund Steimle, in his sermon on Mary and Martha entitled "Martha Missed Something," develops the assertion that Jesus came into Mary and Martha's home bringing God's unexpected kairos-time into their lives. According to Steimle, *kairos-time* is a "moment when we catch a glimpse of what our lives are all about." He reaches into his homiletical culture for several synthetic coordinates to this idea, moments, as he puts it, that are "shaped by God, just for us." Each illustration becomes a type or figure of the meaning of the gospel, which is something still more.

> Years ago, a golden September afternoon in the Pocono mountains here in Pennsylvania, driving along a back road with the top down, the warm sunlight filtering through myriad shades of yellow and gold dripping from the trees. It was so absolutely glorious and gorgeous, it made you want to ache and choke up and cry. A moment of unsurpassed beauty and serenity.
>
> Years later, it was an early morning Eucharist at a seminary chapel in Philadelphia, and as the celebrant placed a little dry wafer of unleavened bread on my tongue with the words, "This is my body," and held the cup to my lips with the words, "This is the New Testament," the words of the ancient creed rang like a peal of bells: "God of God,

---

25. Niebuhr notes that this "more" is "not an afterthought, as it often seems to be for the cultural Christian" (*Christ and Culture*, 144).

26. See Alexander Schmemann, *For the Life of the World* (Crestwood, N.Y.: St. Vladimir's Seminary Press, 1973). According to Schmemann, "The world is meaningful only when it is the 'sacrament' of God's presence" (p. 17). The preacher is like the priest who, in Alexander Schmemann's words, "stands in the center of the world and unifies it . . . both receiving the world from God and offering it to God" (p. 15).

Light of Light, Very God of Very God . . . and became man." A moment in which the incredible miracle of the incarnation happened again, for me. It's the closest I've come to experiencing the immediate presence of God. Maybe.

Or, a rainy afternoon in Massachusetts. We had driven up from New York in a driving rain to see our son away at school. He was about sixteen or seventeen at the time. We were late for the football game, but not caring too much; we were dead sure that the game had been canceled because of the lousy, filthy weather. But when we arrived, one team had just kicked off and a defensive back had taken the kickoff and was slogging his way upfield. At midfield he broke out into the clear, and we suddenly caught the number on his back, number 28. It was Chip, our son, running a kickoff back for a touchdown, Man! We nearly burst with happiness and pride.

A few years later, the three children and I in the front pew of a funeral service for wife and mother who had died in a matter of hours, choking out the hallelujahs of the Easter hymns, clinging to each other in sudden grief and loss, seized by a moment shaped by death, desperately clinging to a God who had turned his face from us, clinging to that God by clinging to each other. It was an exquisite experience of the absence of God, and thus of his presence. In a way more telling, perhaps, than the experience of his presence at the Eucharist.

This example of what Tom Long calls "synechdotal" illustration[27] is a good representation of the synthetic style of cultural coding. Each of Steimle's experiences is a type or figure of his meaning. Emanating from his homiletical culture of upper-middle-class life, which in this instance combines subcultures of nature, leisure, family, sports, education, automobiles, and the church, these experiences *are* the meaning he is conveying, and yet his meaning is something more. The meaning of the sermon is not something else, something better, or totally beyond these experiences; it is, rather, in close and clear continuity with these experiences, taking off from this cultural and experiential ground and flying still further.

Another technique of the synthetic style is what David Buttrick calls the "language of amplification."[28] This, he says, is a language of "but how much more God," by which the preacher indicates the

27. Thomas Long, *The Witness of Preaching* (Louisville: Westminster/John Knox Press, 1989), 165–72.

28. David Buttrick, *Homiletic: Moves and Structures* (Philadelphia: Fortress Press, 1987), 119.

ultimate inadequacy of an analogy to express the fullness of the gospel.[29] According to Buttrick, "In sermons we may liken God's love to worthy parental love, but, again and again, we qualify the analogy by adding, 'but how much more God's love . . .' We magnify in order to establish a realm of distinction between the human and the divine."[30] This kind of qualification made in relation to the cultural code is a form of metacommunication (communication about communication) in which the preacher says to the congregation, in essence, "This is what I mean, but what I mean is also more than this."

Another synthetic technique is to use the language of interaction. The preacher can struggle with some aspect of the homiletical culture or query it for hints and guesses of the gospel. For instance, Steimle might have wrestled with these experiences for their gospel content. He could have followed each vignette by saying something like, "Was something of God's kairos-time present for me in that moment?" or "I don't know all of what God's kairos-time is, but I wonder if these experiences have brought me as close as I will ever come." In this way, the preacher gets the congregation to bring their own experience into a limited interaction with a preached meaning, but makes no assumption that they can find the whole of that meaning within their own experience.

CONSIDERATIONS

The basic problem with this style is that it can communicate indirectly that the gospel is simply a larger version of the deepest and most significant aspects of human life. In Buttrick's words, "We can produce a God-like-us, but on a larger scale."[31] This style can simply be a subtle remaking of God in our own image.

Another, perhaps deeper problem is the assumption that we can arrive at a perspective on our culture and experience from which we can identify the true nature of things, reflections of God's created order. No perspective on our culture and experience is not historically conditioned and thus partial, fragmentary, and relative. To assume an absolute perspective is again to succumb to the parochialism and potential archaism that plague the identification style.

29. Ibid.
30. Ibid.
31. Ibid.

This style also has a tendency toward sentimentality. Preachers sometimes confuse reaching for depth in human experience and culture with reaching for emotion. Sentimental illustrations are sometimes thought to be coordinates for the meaning of the gospel simply because they evoke tears.

The strength of this style is its emphasis on the importance of the creation as a foundation for redemption. Salvation is within and not beyond the created order.[32] Culture is taken seriously as a locus for God's judgment and grace. This message is important to send in a world in which environmental and ecological issues are increasingly a matter of life and death.

An accompanying message is that deep within our culture and experience is the very image of God. This communicates that both Christians and non-Christians can work together to ensure that God's created order is brought forth and actualized, a very positive message in a specialized and pluralistic society in which common goals and efforts are often obscured.

Conversion Style

In the conversion style, the semantic code exists in a transformative relationship to the cultural code. Like the synthesist, the conversionist is positive about his or her homiletical culture. It is an important and vital part of preaching. Unlike the synthesist who is positive because he or she discovers the meaning of the gospel in a deep aspect of culture, the conversionist is positive because where homiletical meaning encounters culture, culture can become a transformed expression of God's goodness.

The conversionist will usually show some aspect of the meaning of the gospel changing or transforming some aspect of culture or human experience. Illustrations will show Christ, Christians, or clear representatives of the meaning of the gospel involved in a transforming relationship with culture. These representatives will encounter some aspect of the preacher's homiletical culture and critique it propheti-

---

32. In Niebuhr's words, "whatever salvation means beyond creation it does not mean the destruction of the created" (*Christ and Culture,* 143).

cally, redeem it salvifically, or redirect, reinvigorate, and regenerate it spiritually.[33]

In a sermon on the Mary and Martha text at the General Assembly of the Presbyterian Church (USA) in 1986, Joanna Adams highlighted the fact that Luke doesn't tell us the name of the village where Mary and Martha live, or tell us that these are Lazarus's sisters. What Luke is saying, she asserts, is that "This could happen to anybody! This could happen to you!" Semantically, this statement means that Jesus is a "savior" who is "going anywhere he wants to." "And it's always that way with a Lord like that. He's coming to see the Americans, but he's going to see the Russians too. And he's going to see Alan Boesak and Desmond Tutu, but he's going to see the Botha government too. And he's going to come to where the Presbyterians are, but he's also going to go to where the Moral Majority is. He's going to go anywhere he wants to! Thank heavens for that." In her illustration, Jesus (the savior who is going to go anywhere he wants to) enters into the cultures of modern global and religious politics so that we can begin to see an inclusive and expansive gospel transforming these cultures. These cultures are certainly not identified with her meaning; neither are they bearers of some deep, synthetic coordinates to her meaning. Rather, they are sinful human cultures that the meaning of the gospel she is proclaiming is meant to transform and convert.

CONSIDERATIONS

The basic problem that accompanies the conversion style is that it can sometimes seem patronizing or condescending. It is a style for those who have power, not for those without power. Only those who have power can convert or transform. Sermons can communicate the idea that the preacher, individual Christian, or church is the sole prophet, transformer, and guardian of true culture and experience. Only when the preacher introduces a gospel meaning into culture and transforms that culture does culture have the chance to reflect the meaning of the gospel. Culture is gospel-bearing only when it has been converted by the redeeming word of the preacher. The

---

33. Ibid., 209. Niebuhr attributes this idea to Augustine.

preacher's homiletical culture can easily degenerate into a mere setup for conversion. It exists only to demonstrate the transforming power of the preacher's gospel message and thus the power of the preacher.

The great strength of this style is its ability to be positive in its use of culture and experience without making culture and experience bear too much freight in communicating homiletical meaning. Preachers in this style will develop a positive relationship to their homiletical culture, use it critically, and not feel compelled to use it all the time. The cultural code will be used only when it can be brought into a transformational relationship to some aspect of the meaning of the sermon.

This style also has the strength of being critical and dynamic. The conversionist is aware of the strengths and limitations of cultural commitments and is less prone to absolutize or sentimentalize any particular one. The preacher feels free to critique prophetically his or her homiletical culture because critique is part of the transformational process of conversion. Sermonic meaning will be brought into relationship to a broad range of cultural situations, many of which are not native to the preacher but better reflect the transforming power of the Christian message.

We have now examined the two dialectical substyles of cultural coding. Again, these styles are united in distinguishing homiletical meaning from homiletical culture while preserving homiletical culture as both necessary for preaching and as related positively to the communication of homiletical meaning.

The dialectical style in preaching sponsors an intertext of *profound* experience, that is, experience that goes beneath or beyond what is superficial, external, or obvious. The congregation is invited to achieve a profound ordering of responses to (experience of) the Christ event. When homiletical meaning is synthesized with culture, the community becomes aware of latent profound experience. When homiletical meaning converts culture, the gospel actually generates profound experience. Whether synthetic or conversionist, the result of the dialectical style of cultural coding is a sense within the community that the experience of the meaning of the gospel is deep and different than surface experience, located somewhere beneath or beyond even our ideal forms of experience.

At its best, this style of preaching will promote a critical but positive understanding of both culture and experience in the church. People will recognize the unique and generative power of the gospel message, which transcends culture and experience and has the potential to generate new culture and new experience. At the same time they will learn to look critically within their culture and experience for traces of the meaning of the gospel and for potential manifestations of the gospel's transforming power.

NEGOTIATING A HEARING

The dialectical style will appear needlessly complex and elitist to the identificationist. It seems to represent an attempt to remove the meaning of the gospel from people's everyday culture and experience, and from the features of that experience of which they are most aware. In order to negotiate a hearing where identificationist expectations are high, the preacher will need to accentuate the positive dialectical move of synthesis and conversion rather than the negative dialectical move of the search for appropriate meaning coordinates and conversion points in the homiletical culture or the precautionary qualification of what the preacher has found in that search. In other words, the identificationist will need to hear more gospel-culture relationship than gospel-culture disparity if a hearing is to be won for this style. Only on the solidly shaped ground of a gospel-culture relationship can the preacher suggest the tensions and disparities that exist between culture and the meaning of the gospel.

The dialectician will also need to be semantically clear about how culture is being used. A word of metacommunication may be in order to avoid misunderstanding. When an identificationist listener who closely identifies the work of Christ with the work of the Moral Majority hears Joanna Adams refer to Christ "visiting there too," the transformational relationship between Christ and the Moral Majority (the New Right) may be missed unless clarified. The identificationist may come out the door congratulating Joanna Adams for "being someone in this denomination who finally recognizes that the Moral Majority's work is Jesus' work."

For those who separate the gospel and culture more exclusively, the preacher's accent will have to fall on the other side. The dialectician will need to accentuate the negative dialectical move, clearly separating the meaning of the gospel and culture. Positive points of synthesis and conversion will need to follow behind these clear separations and seldom be left unqualified.

Dualist Style

In the dualist style, the difference between the gospel and culture undergirds the preacher's use of culture in preaching. As in the dialectical style, the preacher operates from a suspicion of culture and a conviction that the meaning of the gospel in preaching is something else, something beyond culture. Instead of attempting to achieve some form of dialectical relationship, through either synthesis or conversion, the preacher in this style usually avoids and denies his or her homiletical culture as a locus for the meaning of the sermon. The semantic code and the cultural code are in a parallel but discontinuous relationship. Any actual continuity or deep, integral relationship between the meaning of the sermon and the preacher's homiletical culture is denied.[34] The meaning of the sermon is something else, something very distinct from that culture. To synthesize homiletical meaning and homiletical culture or to convert homiletical culture with homiletical meaning is simply to be sentimental or naively optimistic.

Yet culture is not rejected as meaningless. Although suggesting that Christian meaning can be identified in any way with culture would be improper, culture is ordained by God as the native realm of human life and activity. Culture is accepted as the God-ordained "sphere in which Christ . . . ought to be followed."[35] The homiletical culture is simply a necessary, different, and sometimes alien sphere in which the preacher's homiletical meaning must exist.

For the dualist illustrations, appeals to authorities, anecdotes, and all kinds of cultural information are practical tools in service to the semantic code. No gospel-meaning is *in* the cultural code, in either its surface or deep dimensions. The preacher's homiletical culture is a communicational device, no more and no less. It exists to support

---

34. See on this style Niebuhr's "Christ and Culture in Paradox" type in *Christ and Culture*, 149–89.
35. Ibid., 174.

and vivify the content of the preacher's semantic code in a utilitarian fashion.

Sometimes, when the dualist wants to illustrate the meaning of the gospel, he or she will use what David Buttrick calls "the language of denial."[36] This language is especially likely when analogies are used because analogies tend to imply some form of continuity (identification or coordination) between the meaning of the gospel and human experience. Buttrick points out how the preacher can follow the analogy between the love of God and parental love with a denial: "Even our best loving is not love enough. God's love is different and we have no words to describe God's love."[37] Another form of denial is the language of contrast: "Our loves are full of self-love, but God's love is utterly selfless."[38] Were Edmund Steimle a dualist, he might have accompanied the stories of his experiences of the kairos-time of God with the disclaimer: "Of course, my experiences of kairos-time are nothing like the actual experience of the presence of Christ." Through whatever means possible, dualists are concerned now and again to deflate and relativize their homiletical culture.

Because the preacher's homiletical culture is not identified with the meaning of the gospel, no form of experience is ideal. The dualist would never seize on Maribelle Morgan's "total woman" or Robert Schuller's "possibility thinking" as an ideal form of experience. However, common cultural stereotypes are often tacitly accepted as divinely ordained givens within the cultural sphere in which the preacher's message exists. Although these cultural stereotypes are not equated with that message, neither are they critiqued by that message. They are simply accepted as necessary, universal forms of temporal human activity and dwelling. For this reason, the dualist style sometimes resembles the identificationist style.

In considering the Mary and Martha text, Herbert Lockyer's brief exposition of Martha provides a good example of this aspect of the dualist style: "Knowing Martha as we do, we can be assured of this fact, that whenever Jesus visited Martha's home she never had any

---

36. Buttrick, *Homiletic,* 120.
37. Ibid.
38. Ibid.

need to apologize for untidy rooms, a neglected household, or lack of necessary provisions. To her, home responsibilities were never a drudgery. Martha loved her home, was house-proud, kept it 'spick and span,' and was ever ready to entertain her divine Guest or others seeking a refuge beneath her hospitable roof."[39] Here, and throughout Lockyer's exposition, Martha's character is expressed entirely in the cultural idiom of post–World War II television commercials and programs. Images of untidy rooms, lack of necessary provisions, and women who overcome the drudgery of housework and who keep their houses spick and span provide a way of expressing the relationship between her story and our own experience. For Lockyer, this media-supported culture of domestic servanthood is not necessarily to be identified with the meaning he is presenting. Neither is some profound aspect or level of this culture coordinated with a kernel of his meaning. Reminiscent of Paul's acceptance of political authority, slavery, and Roman economic institutions, this culture is simply accepted as the way things are, as a given for Martha and for all women. Women who keep tidy houses are simply doing what is done in their temporal, cultural condition.

CONSIDERATIONS

This style promotes an intertext of received or *conventional* experience. Experience is a given. Little is expected from it except that it exist and continue. The result of this style of cultural coding is a sense within the community that the meaning of the gospel does not significantly derive from or affect the conventional round of experience. The congregation is invited to adopt a conventional ordering of responses to (experience of) the Christ event. Experience is not equivalent to the meaning of the gospel; no deep level of experience or redeemable quality of experience relates dialectically to the meaning of the gospel. Rather, the gospel, especially in its positive and redemptive dimensions, is addressed to a different order of reality, an experience we do not yet know. Therefore, received patterns of experience, unless they deny or refute the existence and reality of the

39. Herbert Lockyer, *All the Women of the Bible* (Grand Rapids: Zondervan, 1977), 88.

gospel, are to be retained and used to facilitate the communication of the gospel.

The basic problem with the dualist style is precisely this tacit acceptance of the status quo as a given for human experience. Because the preacher's homiletical meaning is distinguished from the preacher's homiletical culture and is addressed to a structure of experience yet to come or beyond our knowing, the preacher can easily become disinterested in his or her homiletical culture, use it uncritically, and accept stereotypes that are theologically and ethically questionable. A form of cultural conservatism can develop that accepts even the most obviously non-Christian activities simply because they are part of the given, the God-ordained temporal order.

This disinterested view toward the homiletical culture often means that the preacher seeks little from the cultural code in preaching except, perhaps, an occasional human interest story to win congregational attention. The preacher will tend to use more in the way of canned illustrations and clichés in sermons. The cultural code is not integral to the gospel message. It is simply a necessary homiletical phenomenon that must be carried along in each sermon and used to the best advantage possible so that the meaning of the sermon might be supported and embellished.

Another problematic tendency in this style is for the preacher to provide illustrative material for negative aspects of the homiletical message only and leave the positive, good news dimensions of the message unenculturated and abstract. Law and judgment are imaged plentifully, whereas grace and redemption are spoken about but seldom rooted in culture and human experience, except in loosely paradigmatic ways.

The strength of this style is that the preacher's homiletical culture is usually unobtrusive and seldom attributed too much significance. The identificationist, synthesist, and conversionist always have the possibility of attributing too much importance to culture and experience in the communication of the gospel. When the dualist is in the pulpit, however, many people will learn to take what the preacher says about his experience or their experience with a grain of salt. They know that these are "just illustrations" or "just ways of communicating what the preacher *really* means." Because culture is not the realm of the absolute, it will not be absolutized.

NEGOTIATING A HEARING

To the identificationist and the dialectician, this style may seem insensitive to culture and experience. Culture is not taken seriously enough in the communication of homiletical meaning. In order to win a hearing, the dualist will need to avoid the careless use of culture in preaching and steer clear of canned illustrations and stereotypes. The dualist can use carefully selected cultural references, accompanied by the language of denial. Also, the dualist can learn to be critical of his or her homiletical culture and make sure that the values and ideology it embodies are not contradictory to the meaning of the gospel that is being preached.

Sectarian Style

In the sectarian style, the meaning of the gospel and non-Christian culture are opposed realities. The wider culture is rejected as antigospel. Christian culture is separated off from secular culture and identified with the inner life of a particular community or sect. The Christian community and its way of life represent a special culture unto itself.

In this style of preaching, the homiletical culture will sometimes be bifurcated into a bad or worldly culture and a good, Christian culture. When the wider culture beyond the sect is encoded, it will be used as a figure for what is bad, evil, negative, and under judgment. When the cultural norms of the sect are referred to, they will be used as a figure for what is good, positive, and representative of God's grace and favor. The good culture of the sect will often be designed to appear closely correspondent to first-century biblical culture.[40] Rules for Christian conduct, moral behavior, attitudes, dress, rituals, clichés, and manners will be drawn from what are considered to be scriptural or early church precedents.

Other authoritative models for the cultural rules and practices of the sectarian community, such as pacifism, feminism, or Marxism,

40. This is true for both fundamentalist preaching and for more radical Anabaptist preaching, such as might follow from a commitment to William Willimon and Stanley Hauerwas's "pre-Constantinian" image of the church in *Resident Aliens: Life in the Christian Colony* (Nashville: Abingdon Press, 1989).

can also be used, sometimes with biblical legitimation.[41] However, only minority models for culture will produce sectarian preaching, models that are, like biblical culture, disenfranchised, alien, and different from status quo or worldly culture today. Once a disenfranchised culture achieves mainstream cultural status, even as an older traditional culture, the sectarian style becomes identification style. Jerry Falwell, for instance, attempts a sectarian style by presenting the "traditional family" as if it were a disenfranchised subculture. In fact, however, this culture of the traditional family is still very much a mainstream, middle-class subculture in America. For this reason, Falwell is an identificationist, not a sectarian preacher.

Sectarian preaching is often catechetical. Its purpose is the socialization of good Christian culture and the critical distinction of that culture from bad, worldly culture. The relationship between the semantic code and the cultural code, therefore, is definitional: the semantic code is used to define the content and boundaries of Christian culture. Rather than identifying the preacher's homiletical culture with the preacher's homiletical meaning, using that culture as a point of meaning synthesis or meaning conversion, or uncritically using it as a communication tool, it is used as a means of distinguishing Christian culture from non-Christian culture and of teaching rules for distinctive Christian living.

In a sectarian sermon on Mary and Martha, the congregation hears something like this:

> The world is so full of people going everywhere, but going nowhere really—busybodies, like Martha, unable to see the forest for the trees, lost in daily activities: entertaining, garden clubs, chores, bargain hunting. The world is seductive. It seems to be full of meaning and life, but it breeds misery and spiritual death. Jesus invites Martha, and invites us, to forsake this busybody, material world and put adoration and devotion to Christ first. Mary has chosen the "good portion," forsaking the world and seeking out the face of Jesus in worship, praise, and adoration.

41. As Niebuhr points out, "Radical Christians are always making use of the culture, or parts of the culture, which ostensibly they reject" (*Christ and Culture,* 69). "They can withdraw from its more obvious institutions and expressions; but for the most part they can only select—and modify under Christ's authority—something they have received through the mediation of society" (p. 70).

If the preacher's homiletical culture is rooted in the Marxist cultural idiom, the congregation hears something like this:

> Martha prepares her dinner. She is a slave to a system and doesn't know it. She is a cog in a social machine and lets herself become its instrument. "Send Mary back to work!" she says. "Tell her to help me!" But Mary is free. She is like Juanita, a member of a base community in Brazil, who is learning that she has dignity and self-worth and power. She is finding in Jesus the power to break free from the machine, to challenge the system that has kept her in her place. Her relationship to Christ enables her to disobey the laws and customs of her society and to become a model of Christian liberation.

In both cases the preacher is using the distinction between Martha and Mary as an opportunity to draw out the distinction between a bad majority culture (secular materialism or oppressive capitalism) and a good minority culture (personal pietism or civil disobedience). In both cases the cultural code is a teaching tool for the minority culture's life-style, principles, and rules.

CONSIDERATIONS

The sectarian style promotes an intertext of *separate* experience in the church. Unlike the dualist for whom any experience of the meaning of the gospel is not truly possible in this life, this separate experience is achievable. It is possible within and for the sectarian community of believers. It is a separate reality apart from experience in the round that is achievable only by knowing and living according to the inner laws of the community. The congregation is invited to adopt a separate ordering of responses to (experience of) the Christ event, to become "resident aliens" in the world, and to live in "the Christian Colony."[42] The result of this style of cultural coding is a

42. From the title of the book by Stanley Hauerwas and William Willimon previously cited, *Resident Aliens*. In this book, Hauerwas and Willimon cast aside, with little explanation, Niebuhr's categories, indicating that they are dated and not apropos a pluralistic society. I disagree with their assessment of Niebuhr's "all or nothing" view of culture and believe that, *in the pulpit*, a commitment to Hauerwas and Willimon's position will yield a revisionist form of sectarian thought, comparable in many ways with the thought of Hans Frei, from whom Hauerwas learned his literary critical skills, and George Lindbeck, whose "cultural-linguistic" theology is also a form of sectarian "confessional postmodernism." See also Leslie A. Muray, "Confessional Postmodernism and the Process-Relational Vision," *Process Studies* 18 (1989): 83–95; and Charles Pinches, "Hauerwas Represented: A Response to Muray," *Process Studies* 18 (1989): 95–101, for a provocative debate on this issue, written prior to the publication of *Resident Aliens*.

sense within the community that the meaning of the gospel generates an entirely unique and different form of experience that can be lived (at this time) only within the boundaries of a particular kind of community.

The weakness of this style of preaching is its potential narrowness and exclusivity. It invites people to live in suspicion of the world around them and to adopt a very narrow and particular definition of what is culturally consummate with the gospel message. This narrow definition can easily become a form of legalism that suffuses the grace of the gospel message. Often it has a strong accent on the negative dimensions of the broader culture in order to distance the sectarian community from its cultural surroundings. This tendency can lead to an attitude of fear, superiority, prejudice, or even hatred of the world in which most people live. Then, the sectarian preacher becomes the schismatic preacher whose witness becomes proselytism and harassment.

The only way to overcome this problem is to accentuate the positive dimensions of the alternative Christian culture instead of the negative dimensions of the status quo culture. Preaching should promote a gracious, inclusive vision of Christian culture, one that invites and includes rather than shuns and excludes.

The great strength of this style is its "single-heartedness and sincerity."[43] It promotes clarity about the Christian's relationship with culture and a sincere commitment to the rule and authority of a particular Christian cultural vision. It promotes the kind of uncompromising missionary zeal that, as Niebuhr notes, has led to many of the great political and social reforms throughout the history of the Christian church.[44]

NEGOTIATING A HEARING

As we have noted, the sectarian and identificationist already share a proximate relationship by virtue of their willingness to identify the meaning of the gospel closely with a particular culture. The primary difference is that the identificationist is committed to a status quo culture and the sectarian is commited to a minority or alien culture.

43. Niebuhr, *Christ and Culture,* 66.
44. Ibid., 67–68.

For this reason, these styles of cultural coding are sometimes confused and confusing, especially when a status quo culture is touted as a minority culture, as in the case of Jerry Falwell's culture of the traditional family.

The true sectarian, however, will never be satisfied with any form of status quo cultural identification and will recognize a wolf in sheep's clothing. To give even an inch and allow that any established, traditional, or anticipated common cultural form is even a pale image or weak approximation of the meaning of the gospel is to go too far and concede the gospel into the hands of status quo culture. For this reason, the sectarian may not be able to negotiate a hearing from the identificationist until or unless the sectarian's minority culture is suddenly legitimated as status quo culture, such as, for instance, occurred in the time of Emperor Constantine, or when a revolution ushers in a socialist form of government and sectarian liberation preachers suddenly find themselves identificationists. This kind of thing may happen in the Soviet Union in the near future. Sectarian capitalist preachers in the Christian underground may emerge as identificationists should the Soviet Union adopt a market economy.[45]

The sectarian style rhetorically suggests the possibility of a true Christian culture. For the dialectician and dualist, this change is an impossibility, given the corrupt status of all cultures. In order to win a hearing from the synthesist, conversionist, and dualist, therefore, the sectarian will have to emphasize what they have in common: a commitment to expressing the discontinuity between Christ and the surrounding culture. At the same time, the sectarian will have to paint a powerful, positive picture of the alternative gospel culture, making it attractive and compelling enough to appeal to conversionists and synthesists who may have become disillusioned by failed efforts to bring the gospel into a positive relationship with the surrounding culture.

---

45. For a prelude study of this change from sectarian discourse to status quo discourse among those from the political left of the Congress of People's Deputies, see John S. McClure and Michael Urban, "Discourse, Ideology and Party Formation on the Democratic Left in the USSR," a paper presented at the Fourth World Congress of Soviet and East European Studies in Harrowgate, England, 23 July 1990. This paper will be published by Macmillan Press in a collection of essays from the conference edited by Michael Urban, *Ideology and System Change in the USSR and Eastern Europe.*

APPLYING THE CULTURAL CODE

We have now finished exploring the cultural code and the four ways this code sponsors the textualization of experience in congregations. The fourth layer of our rhetorical schema looks like this:

Cultural Code

Content: References to the broader culture in which the congregation lives its life.
Intertext: Experience; way of ordering one's internal responses to the meaning of the gospel of Jesus Christ.
Styles: Code styles sponsor intertext styles (Table 8).

TABLE 8

Cultural Code and Intertext Styles

Code Style	Sponsors	Intertext Style
Identification		Ideal experience
Dialectical		Profound experience
Dualist		Conventional experience
Sectarian		Separate experience

In this chapter I have indicated that preaching sponsors the intertext of experience in five different styles. Let us look again at a broader analytical process through which the preacher can put this information to intentional, strategic use.

Homiletical Analysis

Begin with an analysis of the content and style of the cultural code in your preaching. Make use of the process and questions suggested earlier in this chapter to analyze your cultural content. Reflect on the way that you use cultural information in preaching to discern your style of cultural coding. (Again, see the next chapter for an example of sermon decoding.) Remember that you can tape your sermons for a few months and transcribe them if you do not use a manuscript.

Congregational Analysis

Although you may have some feel for your congregation's way of relating themselves to the wider culture, you should take time to question members of your congregation to check out your assumptions. You may want to use a congregational retreat or a series of adult classes as a means of gaining responses to the four models I have set forth or to H. Richard Niebuhr's five types of "Christ and culture" relationships. Another helpful tool is the chapter on congregational context in the *Handbook for Congregational Studies*.[46] Although the handbook does not contain a specific tool for analyzing a congregation's relationship to the wider culture, it does provide helpful procedures for determining your congregation's relationship to the wider community's social groups, your congregation's direct and indirect community involvement, and the channels of power and influence that exist within the congregation.[47] The amount and types of such activity are indicators of the congregation's basic relationship to the wider culture.

Theological and Pastoral Analysis

Take time to analyze theologically and pastorally what you are doing and what you want and need to do.

Theological Reflection

Because we have followed Niebuhr's categories fairly closely, reading or rereading *Christ and Culture* may be adequate as a way of enabling theological reflection on your style of cultural coding. After reading Niebuhr's book, think about your own theological commitments. Does your style need to change to reflect your commitments? Ask yourself if your theological commitments are in transition or tend to

---

46. Jackson E. Carroll, Carl S. Dudley, and William McKinney, eds., *Handbook for Congregational Studies* (Nashville: Abingdon Press, 1986), 48–80.
47. See especially the section on "social interaction" (pp. 69–80).

fluctuate. See if you can make a firm personal commitment to one of Niebuhr's models and the corresponding style of cultural coding.

Pastoral Reflection

Look for similarities and contrasts between your current style and the expectations of your congregation. If possible, discuss your findings with members of your congregation so that they can join with you in the process of deciding on your communication strategy.

Ask several questions that will help you think through the pastoral aspects of your findings: What are the significant differences, if any, between my way of encoding culture and my congregation's expectations? In what ways are we similar? What are the differences between the content of my homiletical culture and the content of the congregation's cultural referent for the gospel? What style of cultural coding do we as a congregation need to commit ourselves to at this time? For what reasons?

Conscious Commitment

Commit yourself to a particular style of cultural coding in your preaching. Assess the cultural contents of your sermons regularly to be sure that they are consistent with this style, and use it predominantly if not exclusively.

Again, if this larger process is too much for you to try at this time, reflect on your current style of cultural coding, based on the categories provided in this chapter. Consider ways to improve this style or changes in content you feel you need to make. Think of ways you can negotiate a better hearing for the style to which you are committed. Be sure to ask whether your style is true to your faith commitments and the needs of your congregation.

CONCLUSION

THE CODES AT WORK

In this final chapter we will look at how the codes interrelate and function in preaching. We will use the codes first as a descriptive and analytical schema and then suggest how they can be used in the creation of a sermon.

THE FULL SCHEMA

The completed rhetorical schema is displayed in Table 9.

DECODING:
SERMON ANALYSIS

The homiletical schema can be used now to analyze the rhetorical content and style of sermons. Because we have been using the Mary and Martha story in Luke's Gospel as a case study, we will analyze the sermon "Martha Missed Something" by Edmund Steimle. The sermon text is on the left, and the commentary and encoding are on the right. In the analysis the word *seme*[1] means a unit of meaning or a semantic movement. It can be a block of thought, a portion of an idea, or a further development; a sermon sequence typically has only one major seme.

1. Roland Barthes, *S/Z* (New York: Hill & Wang, 1974), 17. Roland Barthes adapts this word from structuralist linguistics for use in discourse analysis. In linguistics the seme is "the unit of the signifier." In discourse, they are "flickers of meaning" (p. 19).

TABLE 9
Complete Rhetorical Schema

Code	Sponsors	Intertext
Scriptural Code		*Intertext of Anamnesis*
1. Translation		1. Mimetic
2. Transition (traduction)		2. Historical
3. Transposition		3. Representational
4. Transformation		4. Kerygmatic
5. Trajection		5. Heuristic
Semantic Code		*Intertext of Truth*
1. Connotative		1. Disclosive
a. Artistic		a. Epiphanic
b. Conversational		b. Emergent
2. Denotative		2. Conclusive
a. Assertive		a. Decisive
b. Defensive		b. Final
Theosymbolic Code		*Intertext of Worldview*
1. Negative		1. Lack
a. Low		a. Tensive
b. High		b. Oppositional
2. Positive		2. Plenitude
a. Low		a. Equilibrational
b. High		b. Permutational
3. Reversal		3. Iconoclastic
Cultural Code		*Intertext of Experience*
1. Identification		1. Ideal
2. Dialectical		2. Profound
3. Dualist		3. Conventional
4. Sectarian		4. Separate

MARTHA MISSED SOMETHING
Edmund A. Steimle

Sermon	Commentary
There come moments in the lives of all of us of great sorrow, of great joy, of great beauty, or serenity or outrage or insight when time stands still. Past, present, future, all fuse into one, and we have a taste, at least, of what eternity might be like. It is as if they were moments shaped by God just for us. As you look back, it's almost as if you could lift them out of moments which compose our days and taste them again in all the fullness of their zesty flavor.	*Semantic code: seme 1; assertive style; Theosym. code: giver-object-receiver, positive style* The opening sentences assert Steimle's first unit of meaning or seme: that we all have "moments in life." He does not hint at this piece of his larger theme, or bring it into conversation with other hypotheses. He *asserts* that these moments exist and sets out defining them. He then moves immediately into framing this assertion theosymbolically, structuring these moments into our faith story as desired *objects*, "shaped by God just for us." The positive style is indicated because the *object* is clearly given (communicated) by an active and powerful God (*giver*), to everyone (*receivers*). Ascertaining whether this is low- or high-positive style based on one sermon alone is difficult because no clear indication is given whether these moments are signs of great gain and increase in the life of the individual or community (high) or indicate a wholeness to life or restoration of equilibrium (low).
At least, so it has been for me. Years ago, a golden September afternoon in the Pocono Mountains here in Pennsylvania, driving along a back road with the top down, the warm sunlight filtering through myriad shades of yellow and gold dripping from the trees. It was so absolutely glorious and gorgeous, it made you	*Cultural code: personal history, leisure, motoring, nature; synthetic style*

Sermon

Commentary

want to ache and want to choke up and cry. A moment of unsurpassed beauty and serenity.

Years later, it was an early morning Eucharist at a seminary chapel in Philadelphia, and as the celebrant placed a little dry wafer of unleavened bread on my tongue with the words, "This is my body," and held the cup to my lips with the words, "This is the New Testament," the words of the ancient creed rang like a peal of bells, "God of God, Light of Light, Very God of Very God . . . and became man." A moment in which the incredible miracle of the incarnation happened again, for me. It's the closest I've come to experiencing the immediate presence of God. Maybe.

Cultural code: personal history, church, church history, theology; synthetic style

Or, a rainy afternoon in Massachusetts. We had driven up from New York in a driving rain to see our son away at school. He was about sixteen or seventeen at the time. We were late for the football game, but not caring too much; we were dead sure the game had been canceled because of the lousy, filthy weather. But when we arrived, one team had just kicked off and a defensive back had taken the kickoff and was slogging his way upfield. At midfield he broke out into the clear, and we suddenly caught the number on his back, number 28. It was Chip, our son, running a kickoff back for a touchdown, Man! We nearly burst with happiness and pride.

Cultural code: personal history, motoring, education, sports, slang, family; synthetic style

A few years later, the three children and I in the front pew of a

Cultural code: church, family, funeral services; synthetic style

Sermon	Commentary
funeral service for wife and mother who had died in a matter of hours, choking out the hallelujahs of the Easter hymns, clinging to each other in sudden grief and loss, seized by a moment shaped by death, desperately clinging to a God who had turned his face away from us, clinging to that God by clinging to each other. It was an exquisite experience of the absence of God, and thus of his presence. In a way more telling, perhaps, than the experience of his presence in the Eucharist.	As we have already noted in the previous chapter, these illustrations synthesize Steimle's homiletical meaning that "we all have moments . . . shaped by God just for us" with his homiletical culture.
Moments in time when time stands still, and we are sucked up into the juices of life. Moments of deep joy or deep sorrow, of great serenity or great truth breaking in on us.	*Semantic code: seme 1 recapitulated, expanded; assertive style* Note: Steimle reasserts seme 1 cryptically, metaphorically.
In the Greek, as you know, there are two words for time—*chronos* and *kairos*. *Chronos* means time as we normally think of it, of course, as clocks ticking away, or the words of the ancient hymn, "Time like an ever-rolling stream." But *kairos* time speaks of the quality, the significance, the meaning in a moment of time as in, "It's time to speak up," a moment when we catch a glimpse of what our lives are all about. It's as if we stood in such moments with one foot in eternity, for eternity, as someone has suggested, is the essence of time. It's not endless time or the opposite of time. So, in these timeless or time-filled moments, we really stand with one foot in eternity as we glimpse or are seized by the possible meaning of our lives and by what life is all about.	*Semantic code: seme 1a, definition; assertive style; cultural code: timepieces, church hymnody, time clichés; dualist style* Steimle defines the meaning of *kairos time* in order to assert the meaning of seme 1 with more clarity by using cultural references to "ticking clocks" and familiar clichés such as "it's time to speak up" and "one foot in eternity" to support his definition and suggest a conventional (dualist) perception of this meaning. He then reasserts his paradoxical meaning, that these are "timeless or time-filled moments."

Sermon

Now, it's just such a moment that comes to the surface in the story of Mary and Martha, when Jesus came into their house and Mary sat at his feet listening, and Martha, Martha was clattering about in the kitchen doing what must be done when a guest shows up and will probably stay for dinner. Of course, like so many stories in the New Testament, we have so domesticated this story and all but buried it under the fatty layers of familiarity, that we no longer sense the rough edges of it, or the mystery of it either, because this is a far stranger story than it first appears.

One strange thing about it is simply its anonymity. The village is unnamed. The woman, Martha, who welcomes Jesus into her home, is not designated by her relationship to a man—husband, son, father, brother—as was customary. To assume Lazarus was her brother, as some do, is really unwarranted. We simply are not told who these women were or where they lived. Their only significance is that they received Jesus at a time when he was having difficulty being received anywhere. Nor do we know what Jesus was saying to Mary, except that it was teaching, "Torah." And here is another strange circumstance: First of all, it was unthinkable for Martha, a woman without any male relationship apparently, to have invited a man into her house at all. But it was even more unthinkable for Jesus, a rabbi, to teach a woman, to speak to

Commentary

Scriptural code: transition style
Steimle metacommunicates about his approach to Scripture and makes clear that he wants us to go deeper in our interpretation than just a surface reading. He negotiates openly (and negatively) a transitionalist style of encoding Scripture.

Scriptural code: transition/ traduction style

Scriptural code: transition style; theosym.: helper, positive style
Steimle goes on to draw out two transitionalist insights. The first appeals to redaction criticism and notes the anonymity of the women in Luke's Gospel. The second insight appeals to historical-critical knowledge of first-century Jewish law and custom. At the same time, Steimle

Sermon

Commentary

a woman about the ways of God. The law said, "Women cannot speak with scholars even on the street." Moreover, the law said, "May the words of the Torah be burned if they be handed over to a woman. If a man gives his daughter a knowledge of the Torah, it is as though he taught her lechery." Women's liberation had not made much progress in those days.

But the point is, you see, that this is not just a pious little scene, a pious plea for meditation as over against activism. Actually, it undercuts our natural sympathy for Martha, who was simply taking care of the needs of her guest. Once again, you see, as so often in the Gospels, Jesus is breaking with convention, breaking the oral but nevertheless divine law, in order to bring life, to provide a moment for these women in which the meaning of their lives, even what life is all about, might break through.

So something strange and startling is going on here in Martha's house, and Martha missed out on it because, because for one thing, Martha was anxious, so worried about the future that this present moment shaped by God, in defiance of the law of God, was missed.

begins his positive theosymbolic portrayal of Jesus as a *helper* who has power and who brings an entirely different order of reality.

Cultural code: women's liberation; dualist style

Scriptural code: transformation style; semantic code: seme 2; assertive style; theosym.: helper, positive style
Steimle makes the transformational claim that Jesus breaks with convention and uses this insight to enlarge his semantic assertion. The meaning of the sermon now includes a second major unit of meaning or seme: Jesus Christ is the one who "breaks through," as the kairos-bringer. This becomes a strong encoding of theosymbolic content. Jesus is depicted as a strong *helper* who breaks into the normal round of human life and activity, bringing something unique and wonderful.

Scriptural code: translation style; semantic code: seme 3 and seme 3a; assertive style; theosym.: opponent, positive style
Steimle returns to the translationist level of interpretation and picks up an obvious meaning from the text: that Martha was anxious and was missing what Mary was discovering. At the same time, the meaning of the sermon is now developed to include a third seme plus an explanatory seme 3a. The contents of the seman-

Sermon	**Commentary**
	tic code are now: (1) kairos moments happen in our lives; (2) Jesus is the bringer of these moments; and (3) these moments are sometimes missed, (3a) because of anxiety/ worry. This new seme introduces a framing of the theosymbolic *opponent* as anxiety/worry. The positive style is maintained. The opponents are not all-powerful and looming but are things that can cause us to "miss" what God is already giving.
Sound familiar? It is for me. How many life-giving moments do we lose because we are all wrapped up in what the future may bring, worrying about dinner for an unexpected guest or, as in my case, worrying about retirement on a fixed income with only the gloomiest predictions for stopping or even slowing down this damnable inflationary spiral. Or worrying about health, or nursing homes, or kids, or the stock market, or about God knows what all. Meanwhile the possibility of a God-shaped moment slips by in our preoccupation with the future.	*Cultural code: personal history, dinner etiquette, retirement stereotypes, family, economy; synthetic style* Steimle continues using the dualist style and illustrates seme 3a (that we miss kairos moments due to anxiety) as a conventional dimension of life for the nearly retired person.
	Semantic code: seme 3a reiterated; assertive style; scriptural code: translation style Steimle reiterates seme 3a in relation to the obvious meaning of the biblical text.
Martha was anxious, and she was also distracted with much serving. The word is *diakonia*, from which we get our words, *deacon* and *deaconess*. Distracted, busy with the lamb and the rice, the wine and the cheese, and petulant because Mary wasn't busy with the lamb and the rice, and the wine and the cheese, or at least with folding the napkins, for heaven's sake.	*Semantic code: seme 3b, artistic style; scriptural code: translation style and transition style; cultural code: food, etiquette; dualist style* The close proximity of this conjunction *and* with the closure of the previous seme indicates that the semantic code is moving forward. Because Steimle has closely related the scriptural code and the semantic code throughout (banking on expos-

Sermon   **Commentary**

itory expectations?), he now permits
the scriptural code to carry the full
semantic freight, delaying momen-
tarily any clear statement of his
meaning. As seme 3b is delayed, we
listen for a semantic distinction
between anxiety and distraction,
both of which are translational features of the biblical text. The "petu-
lance" of Mary is a brief semantic
attempt to maintain the Martha-
Mary contrast and tension. Steimle
relates these obvious biblical referents to the deeper, transitionalist
research into the word *diakonia*. He
anticipates here the semantic incor-
poration of distracted church people
into his meaning in his next para-
graph. Steimle's dualist cultural coding once again illustrates seme 3b as
a conventional asset of typical middle-class experience. Through the
brief cultural interpolation of "fold-
ing the napkins" into the scriptural
code, Steimle associates Martha's
activity with middle-class American
dinner etiquette.

Sometimes I'm quite sure that the   *Semantic code: seme 3b; assertive*
best way of blocking God out of our   *style; cultural code: cliché, church;*
lives is to keep busy, busy, busy. We   *dualist style; theosymbolic code:*
can even be so busy with prayer, and   *low-positive style*
church services, and church meet-   Steimle now asserts seme 3b, that
ings, and Bible reading, and be so   various distractions can cause us to
busy with all our religious concerns   miss God's kairos moments. He
around the church that there is no   dualistically illustrates this meaning
time for a life-giving moment to hap-   as typical of the "busy, busy, busy"
pen to us.   culture of active church life. Again,
                                        the *opponent* within the theosymbol-
                                        ic code is referenced. Not only is
                                        anxiety a villain in our faith story but
                                        distraction is too.

Sermon	Commentary
In the New Testament, you remember, the scribes and Pharisees, most of them religious people, of course, were so busy interpreting God's law that they missed the divine visitation in Jesus of Nazareth, the life-giving moment which, like Martha, they passed up because they were too busy with other, they thought, more important matters, religious matters. For how does God speak to us, except in such life-giving moments. The Gospels are little more than an array of such individual moments of kairos time.	*Scriptural code: translation style; semantic code: seme 3b expanded; assertive style* Using the obvious dimensions of Martha's busy dinner preparations as a springboard, Steimle identifies her actions with the legalistic distraction of the scribes and Pharisees.
A blind beggar yells for some attention.	*Semantic code: seme 4; assertive style; scriptural code: transformation style; theosym. code: helper, positive style* Steimle smuggles in a fourth seme, the theological assertion that kairos moments are God's way of speaking to us. He introduces evocative, transformational scriptural referents as brief warrants for his assertion, reversing his expository ordering of the codes in order to allow his larger meaning to provoke a new look at the whole of the New Testament. Scripture is presented theosymbolically as a *helper* in our faith story, "an array" of kairos moments that helps us to hear God speak to us.

A tax collector sits in his office interrupted by an intruder saying, unbelievably, "Come on, follow me."

A steward at a wedding, in a snit because the wine has run out.

Ten lepers along the road wailing out their misery but only one grateful for the miraculous cure.

A dead-tired body, beaten, bleeding, stretched out on a couple of beams of wood and nailed there.

A flustered governor, washing his hands of the whole bloody mess.

And then two disciples startled by a stranger on the Emmaus road with a moment of recognition coming in the breaking of bread.

And if you take them all together, these moments of kairos time, adding up to what? Maybe three years? They provide no more than the bar-

Sermon   **Commentary**

est moment in the history of humanity, a moment, however, so crucial for
that history, as you know, we have
divided all the time there is into A.D.
and B.C.

As several have pointed out, there
is something vulgar, downright vulgar about the way in which this God
of the Bible operates. We, of course,
would like to make an abstraction of
him, like a shining, empty cross on
an altar, or like some noble principles for living, or like some timeless
truths, or like some abstract theological formula like "justification by
grace through faith," or like some
vaporous gas permeating all of life,
the abstraction of a life principle. But
he insists on coming in the particular, in the concrete, in a particular
people, in a moment of history, and
worse than that, in a particular male
Jew in a concrete moment of time.
It's downright embarrassing.

*Cultural code: academia, church,
popular theology; dualist style and
synthetic style; semantic code: seme 4
elaborated/defined; assertive style;
theosymbolic code: giver, positive
style*
Steimle further elaborates on seme
4, that kairos moments are God's
speaking to us, providing further
warrants for this idea by referring to
the culture of academia, "as some
have pointed out," and the idea that
God comes "in the particular" as
opposed to abstract ideas about
God's character. His next cultural
references are synthetic, indicating
particular aspects of a "church of
abstractions" that are synthetic coordinates for his meaning ("a shining,
empty cross on an altar"). Theosymbolically, Steimle is contributing to
our positive image of the *giver* as a
kairos-giving God.

And Mary, Mary, sitting there at
his feet listening, had the wit to listen while Martha is too anxious and
distracted with her lamb and rice and
wine and cheese to notice.

Pay attention, for God's sake, to
these moments which seize you when
they come, whether of great beauty
or deep sorrow, moments of sudden
awareness, moments of great joy.
Oh, go to church, say your prayers,
read your Bibles, of course. But
those moments of prayer and wor-

*Scriptural code: translationist style;
semantic code: seme 5; assertive
style; theosymbolic code: subject;
positive style; cultural code: food,
etiquette, church, daily life in middle
America; dualist style*
Steimle again uses his scriptural code
to begin the introduction of a new
seme (5), this time the positive assertion that we can and should listen
(pay attention) for "God's moments." He indicates conventional
arenas of culture and experience

Sermon

ship and study are useful chiefly to sensitize you to the possibility of other moments when you are not in church and your hands are not folded, when God wants to speak to you. Moments when you will stand with one foot in eternity, and you may become aware what your life is all about, even of what life, itself, is all about. Seized by moments shaped by God, for you.

And when they come, as they will, they do for all of us, never mind the lamb and the rice, the wine and the cheese. Never mind the bills, and the meetings, and the housework, and the office politics, and the shopping, and the running noses needing to be wiped. And, pay attention, for Mary has chosen the good portion which shall not be taken away from her.

On Christmas Eve most children live for the moment when they can open their presents, so excited they are practically wetting their pants. In this sense we all live a bit like children. So many presents for us still to be opened, for in a world with God we never know. We never know what will happen or when. It would be tragic, wouldn't it, to miss it when it comes.

Commentary

where we can/should do so by appealing to the homiletical culture of daily life in middle America— "housework," "office politics," "shopping," etc.—that must be abandoned when such moments arrive. He also takes time to qualify semantically his negative indictment of the "busyness" of church life. Also, by now, because of previous cultural associations, when we hear about Martha's dinner, we think of our own dinners.

Cultural code: holidays; synthetic style; semantic code: semes 1–5 summarized, seme 6; artistic style; theosymbolic code: subject and object; positive style
Steimle reasserts his broader theme in such a way that, although some of his minor semes drop out, his major semes are still summarized. What is left is: God's kairos moments can happen at any time; don't miss them! What falls out is: seme 2, "Jesus is the kairos bringer"; seme 3a, "Anxiety/worry causes us to miss kairos moments"; seme 3b, "Distraction (even church work) causes us to miss kairos moments"; and seme 4, "Kairos moments are God's way of speaking to us." What we are left with are essentially seme 1, "We all

Sermon   **Commentary**

have kairos moments"; and seme 5, "Don't miss them." Steimle hints at a sixth seme. He uses the cultural referent of a child's Christmas expectation to indicate the attitude that is necessary if we are not to miss kairos moments. He delays this meaning, however, such that it does not fully achieve assertive status. In other words, he never says, "We must have an attitude of expectation if we are not to miss these moments." He simply compares us to children at Christmas and hints at a further meaning, located somewhere within the image of excited children, provoking the thought, "That's how we are to live in order not to miss kairos moments." Theosymbolically, he images positively an expectant *subject* anticipating an *object* that has already been given but not yet received.

Our decoding of this sermon reveals several things.

1. Scriptural code. Steimle negotiates a transitional/transformational style but uses it only to establish his second seme, that Jesus is the kairos bringer. Otherwise, his use of Scripture is translationist. He permits the semantic code to lead in establishing sequential movement some of the time and permits the scriptural code to lead the semantic code at other points.

2. Semantic code. Although his semantic style could seem conversational because of the quick and constant use of cultural coding in relation to his ideas, Steimle is assertive for the most part and uses definitions and appeals to authority at several points to promote clarity and thematic definition. He does incorporate two instances of artistic style, especially at the end as he delays semantic closure by suggesting quickly a sixth seme through the use of an illustration. The sermon contains a great deal of semantic content, and some of the middle semes lose rhetorical power, especially after his closing illustration fails to include them.

3. Theosymbolic code. His style is positive, accentuating an object given and received. This code is very complete. Most major actants in the faith story receive some deliberate attention in this sermon. The movement of the sermon is from the axis of communication ($G{\rightarrow}O{\rightarrow}R$: God giving kairos moments to everyone) to the axis of volition ($S{\rightarrow}O$: subjects who are missing these moments can overcome the opponent and receive them).

4. Cultural code. Steimle uses principally a mixture of dualist and synthetic styles of cultural coding in this sermon. All of his illustrations are taken from either his personal experience or from the various subcultures of middle-class and upper-middle-class America.

ENCODING:
SERMON PREPARATION

In order to see how the codes can be put to work in the preparation of sermons as well as in the analysis of sermons, we will now reverse the coding process. Prepare a *rhetorical worksheet* to use as a grid for the preparation of sermons by listing sequences across the top of a sheet of paper and the codes (theosymbolic, semantic, cultural, and scriptural) down one side. Using an eleven-inch by fourteen-inch sheet of paper turned sideways will give you enough space to jot in your ideas, illustrations, scriptural information, and theological references. The rhetorical worksheet is to be used as a final stage in your sermon preparation process, after you have done your exegesis and just before you write your manuscript or outline. You may want to use the worksheet itself as an outline.

Table 10 shows what Edmund Steimle's sermon would have looked like on a rhetorical worksheet.

TABLE 10
Rhetorical Worksheet

Code	Sequence 1	Sequence 2	Sequence 3
Theo-symbolic	*Object:* Kairos moments	*Helper:* Jesus, bringer of kairos moments	*Opponent:* Things that cause us to miss kairos moments

Semantic	*Seme 1:* We all have moments shaped by God for us.
	a. Time definitions:
	  1. Chronos
	  2. Kairos
		Seme 2: Jesus is the kairos bringer.	*Seme 3:* And kairos moments are often missed.
			a. Anxiety
			b. Distraction

Cultural	1. Pocono trip
	  Eucharist
	  Chip's touchdown
	  Funeral service
	
	a. Clocks ticking
	  "Time like an
	  ever-rolling stream"
	  "It's time to speak up"
		Women's liberation	a. Dinner preparations, retirement, inflation, health, nursing homes, kids, stock market
			
			b. Serving dinner, "busy, busy, busy," prayer, church services, meetings, Bible reading

Scriptural		Strangeness of text, anonymity Jesus breaking with convention and law, teaching woman	Martha a. Anxious b. Distracted Diakonia—word study Pharisees—busyness

TABLE 10
Rhetorical Worksheet

Code	Sequence 4	Sequence 5	Sequence 6
Theo-symbolic	*Helper:* Scripture as kairos moments *Giver:* God of the particular	*Subject:* Mary, those who "pay attention"	*Subject → Object* Axis of quest
Semantic	*Seme 4:* Kairos moments are God's way of speaking to us Proofs: a. Scripture b. Theology	*Seme 5:* We can and should "pay attention" for kairos moments a. Prayer/Bible study can sensitize us to kairos moments.	*Semes 1–5:* Summary *Seme 6:* Live life in expectation of kairos moments.
Cultural	God of particulars or God as abstraction, vaporous gas	Shopping, work, bills, meetings, running noses	Christmas analogy
Scriptural	Examples: blind beggar, tax collector, steward, ten lepers, crucifixion, Pilate, Emmaus road	Mary contrasted with Martha	

As you can see, you will write shorthand notes to yourself on the rhetorical worksheet to indicate the content you plan to incorporate into each of the four codes. In some sequences, you may not have any content for one code. You can see in Edmund Steimle's sermon that the scriptural code is missing from sequences 1 and 6 (the introduction and conclusion). This may be a necessity in some cases. I encourage students to activate all four codes in each sequence if possible.

Before you write your sermon or create your outline, look at your codes on the rhetorical worksheet. Reflect on your theosymbolic code. Which part of the congregation's faith story are you addressing with this sermon? Are you sure that you are saying what you want to say theologically? Examine the semantic code to see if the meaning of your sermon is clear and well ordered. If you are stringing together several assertions, as Steimle does, are they connected by a compelling logic or relationship? Are you trying to do too much? Look at the cultural code. Does it reflect your style and commitments? Is it narrow and parochial? What are the stereotypes and ideological commitments you are communicating? Are they contradictory to your overall message? What about the scriptural code? Are your scriptural insights truly integral to your sermon? Do you need to negotiate a hearing for your style or is it clear?

Look also at the worksheet for its sense of balance and proportion. Is it too heavily weighted in one place? Is it too sparse in another? Think of your sermon as you might think of a musical score. When a crescendo is needed, more and louder notes will be played; when a decrescendo is called for, fewer and softer notes will be played.

Once your worksheet is ready, the time has come to write your outline or manuscript. In this process, you will order the codes within each sequence and decide on the best strategy to communicate each sequence, based on your style and the material you are trying to communicate.

Relationship Perspective

As you begin to outline or write your sermon, using the rhetorical worksheet, ask yourself the questions, Where do I start? Where do I go next? What is the last thing I should do before I move from one sequence to the next? These questions mean that you must now consider what kind of relationships you want to establish between the codes in your preaching.

Code style commitments will usually dictate the kinds of relationships you tend to establish between the codes. We have already seen how styles of cultural coding are dependent on the preacher's understanding of the relationship between the cultural and semantic contents of sermons. These relationships show up in the ordering of the codes as well. For instance, if you are committed to an identificationist style of encoding culture, you will use your cultural and semantic codes almost interchangeably. If you are committed to a synthetic or conversionist style, you will be comfortable letting your cultural code lead the semantic code in positing meaning; if you are a dualist or sectarian, you will be more likely to let the semantic code have priority over the cultural code.

Many other probable relationships between the codes are rooted in stylistic commitments. For instance, if you have a trajectionist style of encoding Scripture, you will be more likely to bring the scriptural code in after your cultural code or semantic code has established the realm of culture or issue in which the meaning of the Scripture is to be discovered. If you are committed to an artistic or conversational semantic style, you will be more likely to let the cultural code or scriptural code suggest your meaning before you offer semantic hints or hypotheses. If you have an assertive or defensive style, you will be more likely to let the semantic code have priority in the ordering of the codes and to bring the cultural and scriptural codes in behind it as warrants and proofs.

At the same time, commitments to popular subgenres of preaching will also influence the relationships you tend to establish between the codes. The relationship between codes is fundamental to expository, doctrinal, topical, life-situation, narrative, and inductive preaching. Some popular subgenres of preaching accentuate a particular type of semantic content, for example, social, pastoral, therapeutic, and liturgical. Expository, doctrinal, topical, life-situation, narrative, and inductive genres tend to accentuate particular relationships between the codes and the weighting of one or two codes more than others in preaching. For instance, teaching sermons and doctrinal sermons typically accentuate the scriptural, theosymbolic, and semantic codes at the expense of the cultural code. Likewise, expository preachers tend to highlight the derivative relationship between the semantic code and the scriptural code. If, in each sermon sequence, the semantic code leads the scriptural code in the expression of this derivative relationship, we may call the preacher *thematic-expository*. If the scriptural code leads the way, we may call the preacher *textual-expository*, or *verse-by-verse expository*. In some models of life-situation, narrative,[2] and inductive preaching, the cultural code is weighted more strongly or given priority in ordering the relationship between the codes.

Nevertheless, the rhetorical relationships that exist between the codes are not all that define these popular subgenres of preaching. Proponents of the different genres will be quick to note that an entire homiletical mind-set accompanies each genre. A genre of preaching includes commitments that reach behind the rhetoric of the preacher's sermons into the very conception of preaching itself. Still, at the level of sermon rhetoric—of what is said and heard— clearly these popular preaching genres accentuate particular relationships between the four codes.

We can perhaps see these commitments to certain popular genres in Edmund Steimle's sermon. Note, for instance, how Steimle accentuates the derivative use of Scripture. In some places he is textual-expository, permitting the scriptural code to lead the way and suggest his semantic content before he actually asserts it. In other places, he gives priority to his semantic code. He begins his sermon with an assertion, moving slowly toward the scriptural referencing for that assertion. He combines thematic-expository and textual-expository approaches very effectively.

He could easily have begun the sermon, however, with the cultural code by telling his three kairos stories: "Years ago, a golden September afternoon in the Pocono Mountains here in Pennsylvania, driving

---

2. This does not necessarily apply to narrative approaches to preaching such as Lowry's that use narrative at the level of "plot." I am speaking here of narrative approaches that accentuate storytelling within the sermon or sermons as stories. See especially Richard A. Jensen, *Telling the Story: Variety and Imagination in Preaching* (Minneapolis: Augsburg Publishing House, 1980).

along a back road with the top down . . ." After the stories, he could have moved to his semantic code: "There come moments in the lives of all of us of great sorrow, of great joy, of great beauty, or serenity or outrage or insight when time stands still . . ." According to our schema, this approach would have been semantically artistic. It would have delayed the statement of his meaning and gotten the hearer on the hook and scanning for meaning. In terms of popular genres of preaching, he would perhaps appear to be more of a life-situation or inductive preacher.

We can easily see how a preacher's commitments to a particular popular homiletical genre can influence the relationships that are established between the codes in preaching. If a preacher has been taught one of these as the best way to preach or has learned preaching by emulating and modeling a popular genre, these commitments will affect the preacher's ordering of the codes of preaching.

THE POSSIBILITY OF
HYBRID GENRES

Having explored the codes in some depth, we can ask ourselves if new, hybrid homiletical genres are suggested by novel juxtapositions of code styles with popular models of relating the codes. For instance, what do you call an expository preacher whose style of encoding Scripture is transpositionist or trajectionist? What do you call a teaching or doctrinal preacher whose semantic style is connotative? What do you call a life-situation preacher whose style of cultural coding is sectarian?

Popular genres of preaching, which are usually based upon accentuating a particular kind of content or a particular ordering of the codes of preaching, often do not take into account the great variety of styles that can exist for each code. In this book we have provided a schema for discerning these code styles. We can now imagine hybrid genres of preaching based not only on the variations in the content and the relationships that exist between the codes but also on the juxtaposition of a variety of code styles.

I am in favor of putting popular genres on hold and letting theological and pastoral commitments to particular code styles and particular kinds of content dominate decisions regarding the relationships that are established between the codes and the definition of sermon genres. Preachers can then put together their own homiletical approach and take into consideration the impact of their code styles on traditional homiletical genres and the possibility that their homiletical subgenre will be a hybrid genre that does not exactly fit a traditional or popular mold.

Consider, for instance, how dissimilar several expository preachers' sermons would be based on these code style variations. I have selected combinations in this instance that seem to fit well together and would work to support popular expository approaches to preaching.[3]

Scriptural Style	Semantic Style	Theosymbolic Style	Cultural Style
1. Translation	Defensive	High-positive	Identification
2. Transition	Assertive	High-negative	Dialectical
3. Transformation	Assertive	Low-positive	Dialectical

Now imagine what several expository preachers' sermons would be like when the combination of code styles is more provocative and begins to push the limits of the expository genre:

Scriptural Style	Semantic Style	Theosymbolic Style	Cultural Style
1. Translation	Artistic	Low-negative	Dialectical
2. Transposition	Artistic	Low-positive	Sectarian
3. Trajection	Conversational	Low-positive	Dialectical

We could do the same kind of style-mixing for nearly every traditional genre of preaching. When we do this, we discover hybrid styles that barely match traditional expectations within each classical genre. Using the codes to explain these uniquenesses will help preachers to understand themselves better and get a handle on their genre and style without feeling that they have to fit a preset mold that seems to be someone else's conception of what constitutes a particular genre of preaching.

---

3. See especially Haddon W. Robinson, *Biblical Preaching: The Development and Delivery of Expository Messages* (Grand Rapids: Baker Book House, 1980).

SERMON SEQUENCING

As we indicated in the introduction, sermon sequences are indicated by the introduction and sustaining of new content in one or more codes. Each sequence contains shifts between and among codes. Flickers of the presence of several codes may occur in each sermon sequence. We have begun to move on to a new sequence when a particular code leads the way, indicating the presence of new semantic content. Usually, the other codes will follow suit and parallel the lead code with similar content. In most cases it is the semantic code or the particular "meaning" that is being developed in a sequence that will provide a kind of rhetorical boundary for a particular sequence, even though the semantic code may not flicker at the linear boundaries of the sequence (beginning and end) but somewhere in the middle of the sequence itself.

The tendency of any rhetorical theory of homiletics is to prescribe so many sentences of this and so many sentences of that per "point," "move," or "thought block." Various criteria are set for each prescriptive formula: communication theory; the shape of the biblical text; the organic, inner design of your sermon idea; genre commitments, and so on. Considering once again that preaching is not a tactical, one-time public speaking event but a strategic, repeated genre of communication that is negotiated in congregational contexts, we can offer the preacher no such prescription. As a preacher pieces together his or her homiletical style, certain tendencies in the ordering of the codes will emerge that correspond to code style commitments. The only prescription for ordering the relationship between the codes is that the preacher become intentional and strategic in both the content and style of sermon coding and then ask what this approach means for the ordering of sermon codes.

In order to illustrate sermon sequencing without prescribing a narrow format, let me resort to an analogy that the current era of electronic music has set before us. Recently I purchased what electronic musicians call a "digital sequencer-synthesizer." It consists of a keyboard, floppy disk drive, three built-in oscillators, and an eight-track digital sequencer. It really amounts to an eight-track mini recording studio.

It works like this: First, you decide what kind of music you are making. Is it jazz, rock, rhythm and blues, classical, fusion, country? You will want to spend some time conceptualizing the melody and rhythm and perhaps chart on paper the various sequences or movements of the musical piece you are composing. Finally, you decide what instruments you will use and copy them from your floppy disk into the sequencer's memory. Now you are ready to create your first sequence, which is accomplished by recording a rhythm track, which could be drums, a simple melody line, or a set of harmonious chords. This initial sequence may last for only sixteen bars or so. Once this rhythm track is recorded, you begin to add other tracks on top of it, up to eight tracks, until you have created a complete sequence, perhaps including drums, violins, piano, brass, harp, woodwinds, and bass, all of which are neatly stored on floppy disk. Then, you save this sequence as "sequence one" of a particular song on your floppy disk and move on to record the next sequence in the song. In the next sequence you must go back and pick up the basic rhythm and style of the rhythm track from the previous sequence and carry it through on the other tracks as well. You may change volumes, instruments, rhythms, and other variables as you move from sequence to sequence and take the song through various changes in each sequence until at last you have a complete song recorded on floppy disk. You can then play back the entire song, edit it, discard sequences, and change sequences, until you are satisfied.

Digital sequencing can be an analogy for sermon sequencing. First, you decide what kind of sermon you are creating—can we think of kinds of preaching as analogous to jazz, blues, and classical? In other words, remember the code styles (for instance, translation, assertive, high-positive, identificationist) to which you are committed and any kind of popular or traditional ordering of the codes (for instance, expository) that you desire. Then decide what code content (instruments) you will use, fill out your rhetorical worksheet, and look at the whole worksheet for its consistency and comprehensiveness. At that point you are ready to begin your first sequence. Within each sequence encode a lead code (rhythm track). A textual-expository preacher, for instance, may want to begin with the scriptural code. An artistic semantic stylist will perhaps let the cultural code or scriptural code lead the way in each sequence. Instead of eight codes (tracks) per sequence, you have four codes to fill in around this lead code. Be sure that each new sequence relates to the previous sequence in style (translation, assertive, high-positive, identification-ist) and code content. When you have finished the sermon, go back and edit it, discarding pieces of codes or sequences, editing sequences, and changing sequences until you are satisfied.

"Making sermons," then, is a matter of *sequencing* sermons; sermon sequences are made up of the flickering of a possible four codes, arranged in ways that suit your code styles and the kinds of relationships you desire to establish between the codes. Of the many ways of sequencing sermons, some push the boundaries of popular generic types but remain true to your style of coding sermons. Just as Steimle's sermon seems to represent several popular genres of preaching all at once, so your preaching will also seem to become a mixture of these stock genres. The codes, however, will provide you with a theoretical handle on what you are doing and a way of being theologically, pastorally, and homiletically consistent and strategic.

TAKING INVENTORY
OF ONE'S STYLE

In this book, I have provided the reader with a rhetorical schema to use, given a variety of understandings of preaching. As I said earlier, the rhetorical schema is meant to help readers organize the diverse verbal components of their preaching so that they can be more strategically effective for their particular congregations. I have tried to provide a schema that will be useful to preachers who have widely different homiletical profiles and diverse theological backgrounds, conceptions of preaching, pastoral and social contexts, and approaches to the biblical material.

At the very least, this schema will help both homileticians and students of preaching to understand the rhetorical components of preaching in a way that will sensitize them to both the strengths and weaknesses of very different kinds of sermons. As I mentioned before, I hope that the reader will see that one rhetorical strategy does not suit all preachers or contexts for preaching and that hybrid strategies are not only possible but also probable and necessary, given different kinds of preachers and different kinds of preaching contexts. I also hope that the reader understands that all rhetorical strategies for preaching gain more depth and breadth when they are implemented intentionally and strategically.

I believe that this book can promote variety in preaching at the same time that it deepens the reader's consciousness of what he or she is doing in sermon preparation. I am committed to the fact that preachers need not be limited in their homiletical style. A preacher can and perhaps should learn a variety of rhetorical strategies in order to minister to widely varying churches in a highly pluralistic age. Perfect fits between preachers and churches are harder and harder to find. For a preacher to expect an entire congregation to change their strategy of hearing in order to accommodate his or her style is to expect not to be heard or to receive a partial hearing for perhaps several years in a given congregation. Most preachers do not stay in the same church that long. For this reason, preachers must learn to negotiate a hearing as soon as possible when they change congregations.

At the conclusion of this book, as at the beginning, before me remains the picture of the student who knows what she wants to say and who now wants to know how to "make a sermon." Should she be encouraged to become a clone of me or of some other homiletician or preacher? Should she learn to imitate a popular homiletical approach? Or shall I teach her to think for herself and to become a practical theologian of the pulpit ministry so that she can create her own homiletical strategy from the inside out? Perhaps as we think through the codes of her preaching together, we can begin to work toward the second, and I believe greater, end.

INDEX

Printed in the United States
127037LV00001B/6/A

9 780664 228064